TWAYNE'S WORLD AUTHORS SERIES

A Survey of the World's Literature

Sylvia E. Bowman, Indiana University

GENERAL EDITOR

SPAIN

Gerald E. Wade,
Vanderbilt University

EDITOR

V. Blasco Ibáñez

(*TWAS 235*)

TWAYNE'S WORLD AUTHORS SERIES (TWAS)

The purpose of TWAS is to survey the major writers—novelists, dramatists, historians, poets, philosophers, and critics—of the nations of the world. Among the national literatures covered are those of Australia, Canada, China, Eastern Europe, France, Germany, Greece, Italy, Japan, Latin America, the Netherlands, New Zealand, Poland, Russia, Scandinavia, Spain, and the African nations as well as Hebrew, Yiddish, and Latin Classical literature. This survey is complemented by Twayne's United States Authors Series and English Authors Series.

The intent of each volume in these series is to present a critical-analytical study of the works of the writer; to include biographical and historical material that may be necessary for understanding, appreciation, and critical appraisal of the writer; and to present all material in clear, concise English—but not to vitiate the scholarly content of the work by doing so.

V. Blasco Ibáñez

By A. GROVE DAY
and
EDGAR C. KNOWLTON, JR.
University of Hawaii

Twayne Publishers, Inc. : : New York

To
Mildred M. Knowlton,
whose lifelong devotion to books
has contributed to the completion
of this collaborative venture

ABOUT THE AUTHORS

A. GROVE DAY, Senior Professor of English Emeritus, at the University of Hawaii, has lived in Spain for several years since 1927. He began speaking Spanish during a boyhood in Mexico, and in 1936 published a college reader in that language, *Dispatches of Fernando Cortes from Mexico to Charles V*. He used sixteenth-century Spanish documents to write his historical volume, *Coronado's Quest: The Discovery of the Southwestern States* (1940). Dr. Day served as Smith-Mundt Visiting Professor of American Studies at the University of Barcelona in 1957-58 and Fulbright Professor of American Studies at the University of Madrid in 1961-62. Among some forty books he has written or edited are *James A. Michener* (Twayne's United States Authors Series No. 60) and *Louis Becke* (Twayne's World Authors Series No. 9). He is now engaged in writing two more Twayne volumes on Australian authors.

EDGAR C. KNOWLTON, Jr. studied Spanish at the Middlebury Summer School in Vermont; at the Universidad Autonoma of Guadalajara, Mexico; and at Harvard and Stanford (where he taught as a graduate student). He has resided in Spain and the Philippines, and was Smith-Mundt Visiting Professor at the University of Malaya in 1962-64. He is Professor of European Languages at the University of Hawaii and author of numerous articles in Spanish and Portuguese studies. Dr. Knowlton's translation of Sa de Meneses' epic, *Malaca conquista*, was published by the University of Malaya Press in 1970. He is now writing a volume for Twayne on Argentina's Romantic poet, Esteban Echeverria.

Preface

Most readers around the world can name only two Spanish novelists—Miguel Cervantes, author of *Don Quijote,* and Vicente Blasco Ibáñez, author of *Blood and Sand, The Four Horsemen of the Apocalypse,* and some thirty other volumes of fiction.

Blasco Ibáñez (1867–1928) was a man of action as well as a man of letters. He used the power of his pen to spread widely the multitude of ideas and images that thronged in his mind. Born in the beautiful Mediterranean province of Valencia of staunch, energetic parents from the mountains of Aragón, young Vicente early began to write. As editor of a liberal and anti-establishment newspaper, agitator, translator and publisher of low-priced books on history and philosophy, orator, delegate to the Spanish parliament, and party boss, he was always the vigorous center of a reformist movement; a few veteran "Blasquistas" are still to be met in Valencia. Blasco was not afraid to reveal the many evils he saw in his native land, and for revealing them he was rewarded by prison, execration, and exile.

His travels, which extended farther and farther afield during his lifetime and even included a deluxe cruise around the world, gave him further material for his voluminous writings of many types. He published in all some sixty volumes; their quality, naturally, is uneven, and hence selectivity is demanded of the critic. Of these works, the novels are most likely to survive; for Blasco Ibáñez was a born artist in fiction. He has been dismissed unfairly as the author of early examples of regional realism who became the greedy manufacturer of best sellers. His novels of Valencia are universally and justly lauded; but reviewers who pass along the rubber-stamp opinion that Blasco's novels thereafter show a grave decline have overlooked such solid later achievements as *Blood and Sand, The Four Horsemen of the Apocalypse, Mare*

Nostrum, and the five volumes recalling past glories of the Spanish people.

One of the qualities that made Blasco Ibáñez a world figure—he was the most widely translated author of his generation—was the fact that he was a great European who early recognized the growing importance of the Americas. He traveled and lectured in the United States and Argentina, and in the latter country, before World War I, spent several years building two cities colonized by emigrating Spaniards.

Our aim herein has been to study an amazingly popular world author, born in Spain more than a century ago, and to help his readers to appreciate the richness of the many fine contributions in his best works. As writers and teachers, we have been as concerned as anyone could be with the eternal need of readers for broader enjoyment of literature based on deeper comprehension.

Our book is a pioneer study, for no solid critical volume on Vicente Blasco Ibáñez appears in any language. Most previous comments that can be found are vitiated by political or partisan loyalties. None is based on our discriminating, chronological rereading of more than thirty volumes in the original Spanish, supplemented by an examination of the stack of commentaries—ranging in tone from academic to idiotic—that accumulated as Blasco's reputation expanded over the globe. Most useful has been the volume of Emilio Gascó Contell, a lifelong friend of Blasco; this biography by Gascó, supplemented by the one by León Roca and a variety of other sources, forms the basis of our first two chapters, giving the story of Blasco's adventurous career in life as well as in literature.

Later chapters cover successively the groups of novels as they fall into obvious periods of development; a chapter on short stories, novelettes, and nonfiction; and a summary chapter that attempts to measure the stature of Blasco Ibáñez as an artist and craftsman, to reveal his theory of literature and methods of composition, and to suggest the many values that he holds for the reader of the latter years of the twentieth century. A number of unexpected difficulties were overcome in the preparation of the Chronology and Selected Bibliography (which presents all important first editions in Spanish and in English translation, and more than a score of annotated references).

Ours has been an extremely pleasant enterprise in collaboration on a

V. BLASCO IBÁÑEZ

bio-critical volume. To have read many books in a foreign language without an admiration, however tempered by professional standards, for the author's work would have been stultifying. Fortunately, both collaborators, who have been colleagues for twenty years, were in full agreement on the most salient judgments. The writing of first drafts was apportioned, but both authors took the opportunity to rewrite any passage, and the responsibility for all is equally assumed.

All translations herein are the work of the authors. Page numbers of passages quoted in the text refer to the three volumes of *Obras completas (Collected Works)* of Vicente Blasco Ibáñez (Madrid, 1946); however, page numbers from *The Will to Live,* which was suppressed by the author in 1904, are taken from the reprinted edition of Madrid in 1953.

The senior author is indebted to many friends in Spain—a country in which he lived for several years at various times between 1927 and 1965—for suggestions and information. He and his wife delighted in following the traces of Blasco Ibáñez around Spain—especially through his native province of Valencia—and viewing many of the scenes so vividly recreated in his novels. The obloquy that still surrounds the figure of antiauthoritarian Blasco, however, demanded caution in carrying on research in Spain, where to many people the name of Blasco is still anathema. Planned celebrations of homage on the occasion of the centennial of Blasco's birth were cancelled even in his natal city.

No center yet exists for studying Spain's most widely read modern author. Few documents survive; Blasco had the exasperating habit of tearing up every letter to him as soon as he had read it. In addition to the usual infuriating defeats suffered by anyone trying to carry on research in Spanish libraries, there is a suspicious lack of printed materials on Blasco even at his alma mater, the University of Valencia—even in the catalog of the National Library in Madrid, supposedly the repository of all copyrighted volumes. Just to name helpful informants would be tactless at this time.

Given the magnitude of the task of writing this book, the efforts of the senior author would probably never have attained completion had he not been able to enlist the invaluable participation of his friend, Dr. Edgar C. Knowlton Jr., versatile professor of European languages, author of critical studies, and resident of various Spanish- or Portuguese-speaking countries. The editorial expertise of Dr. Gerald Wade of Vanderbilt University and the staff of Twayne Publishers, Inc., is gratefully acknowledged.

A. GROVE DAY
Senior Professor of English, Emeritus
University of Hawaii

Contents

Preface

Chronology

1. The Provincial Revolutionary   17

2. Wanderings of a Cosmopolite   29

3. The Early Valencian Novels   42

4. The Later Valencian Novels   57

5. The Novels of Social Protest or Revolt   69

6. The Psychological Novels   80

7. The Cosmopolitan and War Novels   90

8. The Novels of Spanish Glorification   104

9. Short Stories, Novelettes, and Nonfiction   113

10. Anatomy of a Career   123

Notes and References   138

Selected Bibliography   150

Index   159

Chronology

Publication dates of only more important books are here given; for complete list, see Bibliography. Unless otherwise noted, titles are of novels.

1867   January 29: Vicente Blasco Ibáñez born in city of Valencia, of Aragonese parents.

1875   Entered school at Colegio Levantino.

1882   Entered University of Valencia, Faculty of Law. Published story, "La torre de la Boatella" ("The Boatella Tower") in Valencian dialect, in almanac, *Lo Rat-Penat.*

1883   December 8: Ran away to Madrid and acted as "secretary" to aging novelist, Manuel Fernández y González.

1884   February 3: Returned to Valencia to resume study of law at University; began career as agitator for a federal republic.

1888   Began publishing a group of romantic volumes which he later did not wish to have preserved (see Bibliography). October 23: Completed licentiate degree in civil and canonical law.

1890   Exiled himself to Paris to escape prosecution as antimonarchist conspirator.

1891   Returned to Valencia; on November 8 married his first cousin, María Blasco del Cacho; three sons and one daughter were later born to the couple.

1893   Published essays collected in *París: Impresiones de un emigrado (Paris: Impressions of an Emigrant).*

1894   Presentation in Valencia of Blasco's sole drama, *El juez (The Judge).* November 12: First issue of *El Pueblo,* republican daily morning newspaper founded and edited by Blasco; issue contained beginning of serial version of *Arroz y tartana (Rice and a Carriage),* first acknowledged novel and first of series of "Valencian novels."

1895   Blasco imprisoned for a month on charge of lese majesty.

1896   Self-exiled to Italy for supporting cause of Cuban independence; published travel sketches, *En el país del arte (In the Land of Art)*. Published *Flor de mayo (The Mayflower)*, also *Cuentos valencianos (Valencian Tales)*. Returning to Spain, condemned by court-martial to two years in prison; sentence commuted March 28, 1897.

1898   March 27: Elected for first of six terms as deputy from Valencia to Cortes, National Congress. *La barraca (The Cabin)* (serialized in following year in *El Liberal*, important Madrid daily).

1900   *La condenada (The Condemned Woman)*, short stories. *Entre naranjos (Among the Orange Trees)*. Homage to Blasco celebrated in Retiro Park in Madrid.

1901   French translation of *La barraca* published in *La Revue de Paris;* beginning of Blasco's international fame. *Sónnica la cortesana (Sónnica the Courtesan)*.

1902   *Cañas y barro (Reeds and Mud)*.

1903   *La catedral (The Cathedral)*.

1904   *El intruso (The Intruder)*. Moved to Madrid to live.

1905   *La bodega (The Wine Cellar)*. *La horda (The Horde)*.

1906   *La maja desnuda (The Naked Maja)*. Blasco created Chevalier of Legion of Honor; later rose to rank of Commander.

1907   Entire edition of *La voluntad de vivir (The Will to Live)* destroyed by Blasco for fear of injuring a friend's feelings. Deputy from Valencia to Cortes for sixth and last consecutive term. Tour of Europe as far east as Constantinople, resulting in travel book *Oriente (Orient)*.

1908   *Sangre y arena (Blood and Sand)*.

1909   *Los muertos mandan (The Dead Command)*. *Luna Benamor*, novelette and short stories. First trip to South America; lecture tour in Argentina, Paraguay, and Chile.

1910   Travel sketches, *Argentina y sus grandezas (Argentina and Its Grandeurs)*.

1910–   Stay in South America; founded two colonies in Argentina—
1913   Cervantes and Nueva Valencia—which failed as a result of economic depression.

1914   *Los Argonautas (The Argonauts)*, first novel in six years. Returned to Europe just before outbreak of World War I and lived in Paris, strongly supporting Allied cause.

1916   *Los cuatro jinetes del Apocalipsis (The Four Horsemen of the Apocalypse)*, written in Paris.

1918   *Mare Nostrum.* Best-selling record of *The Four Horsemen* in English creates demand for Blasco's other books and for film rights.

1919   *Los enemigos de la mujer (The Enemies of Women).* Residing at Monte Carlo, Blasco was persuaded to make a lecture tour of the United States; received in House of Representatives, awarded honorary doctorate by George Washington University. Stayed in United States from October, 1919, to July, 1920.

1921   *El militarismo mejicano (Mexican Militarism)*, volume of essays resulting from visit to Mexico in that year.

1922   *La tierra de todos (The Land of Everyone). El paraíso de las mujeres (The Paradise of Women).*

1923   *La reina Calafia (Queen Calafia).* Universally acclaimed as an author, Blasco began in October a six-month trip around the world; sketches published in three volumes in 1924–1925 as *La vuelta al mundo de un novelista (A Novelist's Tour of the World).*

1924   *Novelas de la costa azul (Stories of the Côte d'Azur).* Still active as an antimonarchist, Blasco published *Alfonso XIII desenmascarado (Alfonso XIII Unmasked)*, an attack on the Spanish king and the dictatorship of Primo de Rivera.

1925   Wife María died; Blasco made second marriage, to Elena Ortúzar Bulnes, daughter of a Chilean general. *El papa del mar (The Pope of the Sea).*

1926   *A los pies de Venus (At the Feet of Venus).*

1927   *Novelas de amor y de muerte (Stories of Love and Death).*

1928   At work on novel about League of Nations and the world of the future, to be called *The Fifth Horseman of the Apocalypse,* Blasco died on January 28, eve of his sixty-first birthday, on his large estate at Menton on French Riviera; buried in France.

1929   *En busca del Gran Kan (In Search of the Great Khan)* and *El Caballero de la Virgen (The Knight of the Virgin)* published posthumously.

1930   *El fantasma de las alas de oro (The Phantom with Wings of Gold).*

1931   April 14: The Second Spanish Republic, for which the novelist had conspired and propagandized, proclaimed.

1932   April 14: A memorial tablet was dedicated on the Avenida de

Blasco Ibáñez in Valencia, adjoining the plaza which had previously been named for him.

1933   October 28: Body of Blasco, borne from France by ship to Valencia, greeted with acclaim at port by large crowd and interred with full military honors in city cemetery. Commemorative booklet published by the Excelentísimo Ayuntamiento of Valencia.

CHAPTER 1

The Provincial Revolutionary

VICENTE Blasco Ibáñez was the most widely read Spanish author of his generation, and is the best-known Spanish novelist except for Cervantes.

He rose through tremendous vigor from a childhood in a small provincial shop to a high place as an international figure admired by millions. Born storyteller that he was, he invented no novel more exciting than the chronicle of his own life.

Law student, antimonarchical and anticlerical agitator, social reformer, newspaper editor, political jailbird and exile, six times representative in the national assembly, duelist, publisher, founder of cities in Argentina and Patagonia, historian of World War I, lecturer in the United States, mogul of the movies, lord of a palatial estate on the French Riviera—Blasco Ibáñez in his time played all these roles with fervor.

But from childhood he wrote, and wrote voluminously, with an almost sensual gusto. His collected works run to thirty-six volumes and he published more than a score of others. In all of them his intention was to show Spain to the Spanish and to the rest of the world—to show it in true tones, its misery and cruelty as well as its sturdy endurance and wild heroism, past and present. He and his contemporary, Benito Pérez Galdós, were the two Spanish authors most violently attacked by Spanish critics precisely because they were the writers most devoted to mirroring their homeland with vivid, and often unflattering, veracity.

I A Runaway to Madrid

Blasco Ibáñez was born in 1867 in the city of Valencia, and Valencia was the base from which he set out to conquer the world. To know Blasco, one must know something of Valencia; and from Blasco one can learn best the Valencia of his youth, for some of his greatest novels are set in his native province.

Valencia is still a rather self-satisfied city, "The Pearl of the Levant," lying on a rich alluvial plain cupped by mountains and laved by a Mediterranean as blue as the almost always cloudless sky above it. The people of the region had always been able, by using its natural wealth and beckoning charm, to absorb its conquerors. Phoenicians, Greeks, Carthaginians, Romans, Visigoths, Arabs, Catalans—all had passed that way and had left their traces on the soil and in the features of the inhabitants. The result, in the words of one Valencian, was "a temperament somewhat inconstant, somewhat whimsical, versatile, impressionable, daydreaming." [1]

The city, which in Blasco's boyhood numbered about 150,000 people (it now has grown to a million), was the center of a vast garden of orange trees, rice fields, and truck gardens, and a lively port for fishermen and oceangoing ships alike. In the waterfront cafés, the wine and crusty bread of Valencia were ordered in twenty languages. Despite the hard work required of the inhabitants to extract a livelihood from soil or sea, or to earn pay in a factory, the ordinary Valencian was considered somewhat soft, unvirile in comparison with the folk of such neighboring provinces as Cataluña, where the men "made bread from stones," or from the rocky ravines of Aragón, from which many starving peasants had descended to outwit and outwork the dwellers on the Valencian plain through exercise of greater vigor and determination.

Blasco's first serious novel, *Arroz y tartana (Rice and a Carriage)*, for instance, gives an account in the second chapter of the custom of poor Aragonese peasants of taking a boy child to the market square in Valencia, distracting his attention by pointing out to him the fabled peacock weathervane, and deserting the waif to survive in the hope that a kind Valencian family would take him in and give him the food his parents could not.

Blasco Ibáñez himself was born in Valencia, but he inherited the vigor of Aragón from both parents. Nor was he a nameless waif. His birthplace was a room above a corner grocery kept by those parents in an old neighborhood behind the church of Los Santos Juanes and not far from the main marketplace of the city and the ancient Lonja, the silk exchange.[2]

His birth date was given on the certificate as January 29,[3] and his parents were Gaspar Blasco Teruel of Aguilar de Alfambra and Ramona Ibáñez Martínez of Calatayud, both coming from villages in the Aragonese district of Teruel.[4] According to the custom in Spanish countries, the "middle name" of Vicente Blasco Ibáñez was his patronymic and his "last" name that of his mother's father. Even in later years the author never got accustomed to being addressed by foreigners as "Mr. Ibáñez."

His father, described as "headstrong, robust, large-mouthed, red-faced, brusque, and outspoken," [5] passed on some of these Aragonese traits to his son, but it should not be forgotten that if the novelist's heredity was Aragonese, his early environment was Valencian.

The child was baptized in the nearby church of Los Santos Juanes. His Christian name (Vicente is the Spanish form of Vincent) derived from his mother's aunt Vicenta Martínez, but this choice did no harm to his political career in a city whose patron was the martyred Roman deacon Vincent and whose chief philosopher was St. Vincent Ferrer. The lad was an only son (a daughter was born several years after) and was given a Catholic education at the nearby Escuelas Pías. A picture of him survives showing him marching in the Corpus Christi procession, dressed in the garb of St. John the Baptist. Early indoctrination failed, however, for the boy grew up to be one of history's strongest critics of Spanish Catholicism.

In 1875 the lad—of sturdy build, with big sparkling brown eyes and crisp, curly brown hair—entered the Colegio Levantino, a school where he used to entertain his fellows by telling them stories "made up out of his head." He often played truant, to wander on the beach of Cabañal and talk to fishermen and sailors, or to join the vagrant bands of gutter children that lived like sparrows in the narrow streets of the Old Quarter.

Vicente early showed his talent for literature, however; he wrote a "cloak-and-sword" novel at the age of fourteen in a country villa his father had bought at Burjasot, a setting Blasco used in *Rice and a Carriage*. His first published story, "La torre de la Boatella" ("The Boatella Tower") appeared in November, 1882, written in the Valencian dialect, in *Lo Rat-Penat,* an almanac named for the pensive bat which was on the helmet of the conqueror Jaime I and became an emblem on the arms of Valencia.

Emboldened by this appearance in print, the lad, not yet seventeen and now a student at the venerable University of Valencia (founded in 1500 A.D.), left home and ran away to Madrid, his main luggage the manuscript of a big historical novel. This first venture of the future world traveler did much to broaden his outlook and his politics, but the capital did not welcome him with open arms. Scorned by Madrid editors, young Blasco decided that some day he would do something about recognizing youthful literary talent; later, Editorial Prometeo, the publishing house he founded, fulfilled this goal.

II   *Rise of a Republican*

To keep from starving, Blasco took a post as "secretary" to an aging novelist named Manuel Fernández y González (1821–1888). This writer, whose historical romances rivaled those of Scott and Dumas, had once lived close to penury, although he had published some five hundred novels as well as poetry and plays. He and his young amanuensis would dine on a stale roll and coffee in a cheap café and then walk home to a chilly back room where the old man would dictate for hours his outmoded tales of intrigue. When he dozed off, young Blasco would continue the story himself until the quill fell from his fingers. This apprenticeship left its mark on Blasco's early style, and under this brief but strong influence he published between 1888 and 1892 a dozen romances which later he desired to be forgotten.[6]

During this brief Madrid escapade, from December 8, 1883, to the following February 2, Blasco also found time to make speeches in small political clubs to which he was introduced by friends in his boarding-house on Calle de Segovia. His nickname at these meetings was "El Estudiantito"—"the little scholar." One night he was picked up by the police and taken to the local jail. Preparing to defend himself with an oration that would be sure to make him a martyr to the cause of the federal republic, he was soon deflated by the news that his mother had used this means to get in touch with him and plead with him to return home to Valencia.

Back in the city of his birth, he continued the career of agitator among the various clubs in the suburbs, and continued also his literary outpourings. Before he was seventeen he had published a poem advocating the chopping off of all the crowned heads in Europe, starting in Spain. The criminal court sentenced him to six months in jail, but suspended the sentence because of his youth.

His fiery orations were heard in such neighboring towns as Liria and Pedralba, but somehow he also found time to finish his degree at the University.[7] He seldom attended classes—a fact that pleased the authorities, for whenever he appeared, the beadles would warn each other that the "stormy petrel" was back and that more political riots would soon break out in the patio of the Faculty of Law.

One of Vicente's ancestors had been a heroic curate, and the young man's mother desired that he also might enter the priesthood. He himself yearned to become a naval captain, but was unable to grasp enough mathematics to pass the navigation tests. His love of the sea is, however, revealed in more than one novel, such as *Flor de mayo (The Mayflower)* and *Mare Nostrum.*

For want of any other devotion, Blasco took his degree in law, reminding one of the old saying: "Assume that every Spaniard is a lawyer until he proves himself otherwise." By dint of cramming fiercely before the critical examinations, Blasco obtained a licentiate degree in civil and canonical law on October 23, 1888.

His sonorous voice was still upraised, in Castilian as well as Valencian, in speeches advocating social justice. As a sample of his anticlerical opinions, a few lines may be quoted from an address given to a Masonic group in December, 1888, on the occasion of their adoption of a homeless mother and two children:

Ask the Jesuit, the priest, the friar, and in the moment of frank admission when the truth escapes their lips they will tell you that in them (the women and children) they have found the firmest base of their power, and that they have been the weapons that, wielded with skill, have caused the greatest harm to their adversaries. . . . What does this mean? That the woman and the child are still in the power of the curate and the Jesuit, that they still huddle in the cold shadow of the Catholic Church and cross themselves with horror at every sign of progress that justifies humanity. . . . To this end they utilize two means: the confession and the school.[8]

In 1890, accused of causing an uprising against the accession to power of Cánovas del Castillo, Blasco was forced to go into exile. He chose Paris and stayed in a *pension* frequented by other Spanish political exiles, becoming more imbued than ever with the revolutionary spirit. He enjoyed the gay life of the City of Light, read the works of Balzac and Zola, made friends with French politicians, and because he received a monthly income of three hundred pesetas from Valencia was considered by his bohemian chums to be an easy source of a loan.

As the result of an amnesty, Blasco returned to Valencia in July, after a year in France. His devotion to the ideals of that country had strengthened, and he had used the time to write a three-volume *Historia de la revolución española, 1808–1874 (History of the Spanish Revolution, 1808–1874),* which, when it appeared in 1892, made a good deal of money for his Barcelona publisher.

Blasco now decided to settle down and start a family. On November 18, 1891, he married his first cousin, María Blasco del Cacho, an orphan born in 1870 and related to a respectable Valencian family. Her father, Don Rafael Blasco y Moreno, had been a magistrate in Castellón de la Plana as well as a Romantic poet and a noted collector of ceramics. A rather stern, dark woman, María endured Vicente's stormy later career and bore him five children, but incompatibility increased, and before World War I the couple decided to separate.[9]

A collection of essays by Blasco appeared in 1893 which had been written in Paris from August, 1890, to July, 1891, recording his lively impressions for readers of a Spanish paper. In May, 1894, Blasco's first and only drama, *El juez (The Judge)*, was performed with some success in the Teatro Apolo in Valencia, but the opening night was saddened by the death of his mother.

In this critical year 1894, Blasco took an important step and devoted himself wholeheartedly to agitation for community reform and a federal republic. Politics was in his blood. His father had been a devoted Carlist, supporting a strong pretender to the Spanish throne, and the corner where the family shop was located had been the scene of many a local broil.

The typical Spaniard, if politics is "the art of the possible," has an idealistic, apolitical nature, for to him compromise or the acceptance of unfavorable election returns is repugnant. On the other hand, he likes to take a violent stand and, if not always the leader of a one-man party, supports his clan, his province, or his sect without stopping short of duels or the tactics of the guerrilla (a Spanish word). From 1808, when Napoleon broke the principle of royal legitimacy by putting his brother Joseph on the Spanish throne, until 1939, when Spain lay exhausted, having killed a reputed million of her own people in the bloodiest civil war in European history, the country was in a continual turmoil. Thus the young Blasco grew up in a land that imbued everyone with a spirit of fiery partisanship.

III *Duelist, Jailbird, and Orator*

The year after Vicente's birth, Queen Isabel II was overthrown by a revolution and replaced by the provisional government of General Francisco Serrano that produced the Constitution of 1869. In 1870 began the reign of King Amadeus of Savoy, who abdicated in disgust after three years. The Second Carlist War was fought from 1872 to 1876. When young Vicente was seven, the ill-fated First Republic began its chaotic year in power (in eleven months there were four presidents). The experiment collapsed with the restoration of the Bourbons in the person of Alfonso XII, whose death in 1885 plunged Blasco into his career as republican conspirator and political jailbird. While Blasco was in exile in Paris, his young friends in Spain were being conscripted to fight the Moors in Melilla in North Africa. Later, from 1895 to 1898, there was to be revolt in the colony of Cuba, anarchy in Barcelona, and a humiliating war with the United States that resulted in the loss of Puerto Rico and the Philippines, Spain's last overseas colonies, and the demand for a violent shift in the course of Spanish political thought.

In Valencia the people had been aroused to sentiments of political freedom, often going back to the French Revolution. The dream of a republic enunciated by Francisco Pi y Margall appealed to many as a Greco-Roman panacea for all ills. A Valencian recalls an unlettered shoemaker in his neighborhood who, like Blasco Ibáñez, named his first daughter Liberty. The second was named Equality. And when the third arrived, the "freethinker" unabashedly named her Fraternity![10]

Blasco Ibáñez took the step, and published on November 12, 1894, the first issue of a daily morning newspaper of republican leanings, *El Pueblo (The People)*. He was not without experience. He had launched two short-lived literary journals in 1883, and on September 1, 1889, had founded a fiery weekly paper, *La Bandera Federal (The Republican Banner)*. Into *El Pueblo* he sank his entire inheritance, and for it he engaged in editorial labors that would have killed anyone with a smaller reservoir of stamina. This man, later to be accused of meretriciousness and of writing merely to pile up a million dollars, poured all his enthusiasm and cash into a crusading newspaper doomed never to make any money at all. "Blasco Ibáñez ran a grave risk of working like a slave to lose every cent he had in the world," says one commentator. "Those who accuse him of greed and materialism should enter this item on the credit side of his account."[11]

Still under twenty-eight, Vicente Blasco Ibáñez was made of sterner stuff. He was large, heavy-set, with a rugged body, the broad chest of a sailor, and an imperious bearing. His feet were small and his hands aristocratic. His chestnut hair was abundant, with crisp curls above an imposing forehead from which the hair was already receding. His nose was aquiline and his sensual, thick-lipped mouth was covered by a moustache. While editing his newspaper he was the only one of his volunteer staff that sported a curly, pointed beard, which gave him an Arabian look. The glance from his dark brown eyes was quick and took in details with photographic fidelity. One's first impression on meeting him was of coldness, an impression that was replaced by partisan warmth as soon as his sonorous voice boomed out with stirring appeals or enthusiasms. He was fluent, sometimes verbose, in both Castilian and Valencian, and in early speeches did not avoid crudities or even profanity. A born leader of crowds, self-made, self-assured, he indulged in striking gestures that were later to decline into posturing. At all times he seemed impulsive and impatient to achieve overnight the abolition of stupidity, sloth, and ignorance.

Blasco loved to read from boyhood. The book that earliest impressed him was a translation into Spanish of Washington Irving's *Life of Christopher Columbus.* "Everything interests me," he once said, "except mathematics. My true passion is history." [12] One of his achievements was to try to bring good reading to the Spanish people. He founded a publishing house that issued not only his own works, but those of a hundred other writers, mainly European thinkers, which he brought to the public at prices most could afford. Editorial Prometeo, begun in partnership with his friend Francisco Sempere, early started issuing books when the aged press of *El Pueblo* was not otherwise in use. F. Sempere and Co., 10, Calle de Palomar, which later became "El Prometeo" press, published not only all of Blasco's works, including a translation by him of Michelet's *History of the French Revolution,* but many works by Renan, Gorki, Spencer, Tolstoi, Nietzsche, Kropotkin, and dozens of others. The Prometeo imprint on a one-peseta book, the partners hoped, would create a revolution through adult education.

Blasco's main passion, however, was writing. As he once said, he would never abandon the pleasure of composition to indulge any fleshly appetite. Often he would lock himself in his room and fill folio after folio in his scrawling hand for sixteen or eighteen hours at a stretch. Once he wrote for thirty hours, with no pause except to gulp a cup of coffee or to light another Havana cigar.

In 1894 this young Quixote was setting out to realize a finer culture for the city of his birth. Practical in methods, he was idealistic in aims.

Blasco was antireligious in one of the most Catholic cities in the world. Valencia's cathedral was the sacred repository of the true Holy Grail, and within half a mile of it were a dozen other venerable centers of worship. Victor Hugo spoke of "Valencia, with the belfries of its three hundred churches." But Blasco soon became an active Mason—in Europe a strong anticlerical organization.

Blasco was a republican in a city that looked back to the good old days of Jaime I (1208–1276) and Alfonso the Magnanimous (1396–1458). He fought at least a dozen duels with monarchist firebrands. He was wounded several times, but he told his seconds on the field of honor, "I do not fear these bullets, for I am destined for higher things in the world." However, he later regretted such acts of bravado, saying: "When I think that I was wounded, almost mortally, three months before writing *La barraca!*" [13] But he had to prove to his followers that he was afraid of nothing.

Blasco was a radical reformer in a city priding itself on its conventions, and extreme only in its bourgeois moderation. He wanted to advance secular education, juvenile and adult, and as he said: "Since the people cannot ascend to the university, the university must descend to them."[14]

Blasco sought to make a New Athens of a city that was less interested in culture than in the price of fish. True, the first book ever printed in Spain came off the press in Valencia, in 1474, a collection of poems in honor of the Virgin Mary; but its citizens had shown no great desire for reading even the works of their own Vicente Ferrer and Juan Luis Vives. Now, in a province that had produced few authors, Blasco aimed to create a revolution through authorship. Five of his finest novels, those dealing realistically with Valencian life, were written from day to day, to appear serially in the pages of *El Pueblo*.

Fortunately, at this height of his energy, Blasco was equal to the challenge. He formed his own political party. As a result ot taking an active part in the Assembly of Castellón, which in 1903 founded the national Unión Republicana, Blasco was confirmed as chief of the Valencian branch, whose adherents had proudly called themselves Blasquistas, or followers of Blasco. He organized meetings in the city and the region, arousing enthusiasm by his fiery oratory before large groups of fishermen, peasants, and laborers. To his humble rooms at No. 10 Calle Don Juan de Austria, on the floor above the editorial office of *El Pueblo* and the pounding press on the ground floor, Blasco was followed by crowds of workers who demanded one more republican harangue from the balcony by their "Don Visentico."

Since he had sunk all his inheritance in the newspaper, Blasco let his wife feed the family on rice, chard, and fried potatoes. As party leader he tried to conceal his situation, but his daily wear was the same old tweed jacket and blue pants, shiny from sitting at his desk. And he was at that desk most of his waking hours, when not addressing crowds or languishing in the city jail under a charge of sedition.

IV *Hurrah for Madness!*

El Pueblo was virtually a one-man paper, and Blasco's staff consisted merely of a carefree group of young radicals willing to contribute their outpourings without pay. One of them was José Martínez Ruíz, a young law student later to become famed under the pseudonym of "Azorín." But day after day Blasco himself had to meet the deadline by writing the entire issue, from the incendiary opening editorial to the obituaries on the back page. He would take a few telegrams and puff them out into space-filling commentaries, and dictate a chapter or two of his latest novel to serve as a serial.

Here was a newspaper addressed to workingmen, most of whom could not read. The editor tried to elevate the taste of the readers by highbrow articles and translations from European pundits. Its subscription list, at a price of one peseta a month, was pitifully small. It was naturally blacklisted by all advertisers. But somehow *El Pueblo* continued to appear most of the time.

The main interruptions of publication came from its frequent suppression by the government and the jailing of its contributors. Almost every day, the editor or one of his band of writers was hauled off to incarceration in the prison of San Gregorio. For such occasions, a folding cot and a mattress were kept in the office, to be lugged to the jail for the use of a staff member who had been arrested. Blasco himself slept on this cot during the month he spent in San Gregorio in 1895 on a charge of lese majesty. He wrote that he had been arrested no less than thirty times. As he once remarked, "Actually, my only periods of peace and repose in those busy days were those I spent in jail." [15] To avoid a similar servitude, after *El Pueblo* had aroused such popular manifestations against the war opposing the Cuban revolutionaries that Valencia was declared in a state of siege, Blasco fled for three months in 1896 to Italy, where he wrote a book of impressions, *En el país de arte (In the Land of Art)*.

Incautiously, he returned to Valencia. When another commotion broke out against the Civil Guards, he was arrested, since as one officer said, "Not a leaf stirs in Valencia unless Blasco gives the order." The sentence of the court-martial was read to him on September 21 as he stood in candlelight, surrounded by bayonets, in the middle of the prison yard. He was condemned to two years at hard labor in the familiar prison of San Gregorio. With shaven head, wearing the convict's garb of shame, he lived with criminals for many months, obtaining, in this hard way, firsthand material for novels and short stories, such as those in *La condenada (The Condemned Woman)*, 1900.

His sentence was commuted in March, 1897, on condition that he leave Valencia for Madrid and report regularly to the police in that city. But his popularity at home had increased to the point where he was overwhelmingly elected by Valencia on March 27, 1898, to represent it in the National Congress. Thereafter he was to be reelected to this office for five more terms.

His first act was to publish an attack on the government policy in the disastrous war against the United States. Despite his presumed legislative immunity, he was again jailed, to be released only through the efforts of his fellow parliamentarians. In this same critical year he wrote sporadically, for serial publication in his newspaper, *La barraca (The Cabin)*, which many critics have judged to be his finest novel.

Blasco's power as a speaker in the Cortes in 1899 is described by a journalist, Roberto Castrovedo. When Blasco was given the floor by his republican sponsor and idol, the leader Pi y Margall, the hall would wait eagerly. "Blasco, straightening up, arrogant, passed his hand over his handsome brow and approached the platform. His voice, intense and melodious, his noble and unrestrained posture, subdued them all. 'I am from Valencia!' he would begin . . . and the first applause would explode frenetically and *vivas* to Valencia would resound." [16]

Success in national politics did not interrupt Blasco's labors on behalf of his native city. *El Pueblo* carried on a campaign against gambling. The town council was strongly Blasquista. Schools and institutes for laboring people were opened, and much civic progress was made. As a result of his efforts, a municipal orchestra was founded. All his life Blasco was fond of music, especially that of Wagner and Beethoven.[17] As *caudillo* or "boss" of his party, Blasco wrote letters of recommendation, found jobs for constituents, and even handed out cash to needy clients.

But now began a fatal split in the republican party in Valencia that diverted reform efforts to a bitter internecine strife. A wealthy young aristocrat, Rodrigo Soriano Barroeta-Aldamar of San Sebastián, offered to forsake the monarchist party and devote himself to Blasco's cause. Through Blasquista support, Soriano was also elected to represent Valencia in the Cortes.

Insidiously, however, Soriano undermined his leader and attracted to himself the dissidents, the waverers, and the venal. From 1903 to 1907, the party was shattered. Soriano hired a gang of bodyguards and a squad of goons to stir up trouble. Fighting broke out in the streets, and the grim battles between the Blasquistas and the Sorianistas are still recalled by Valencian veterans.

Soriano started a rival newspaper, *El Radical*, and the verbal warfare between it and *El Pueblo* exceeded even the venomous journalism of the American frontier. For example, Blasco built for himself and his family a three-story home on the beach at La Malvarrosa, several miles from his office.[18] Here he sought peace and quiet, for he found himself no longer able to write novels in a city whre he was daily trailed by devoted partisans who clamored for his time. "La Malvarrosa" was built according to Blasco's own design as a model villa suitable for utilizing the beauty and the comforts of the Valencian shore, and could be approached only by rowboat or by a long walk over the dunes. Its furnishings were rather simple, but the Blasco library was thrown open to all subscribers to *El Pueblo*, and in the house many famous visitors were entertained.

The Soriano newspaper began to refer to the bearded Blasco as "The Sultan of La Malvarrosa," hinting that this edifice was financed by graft and was a place of Oriental luxury and vice. To protect himself, Blasco opened all the house, except his writing room on the top floor, to any visitor, who could roam from the colonnaded portico to the tiled farm-style kitchen and observe the lack of a harem or an opium den.

One visitor who forced his way up to the studio turned out to be "El Mosca" or "The Fly," Soriano's chief thug, who offered for a small sum to assassinate his patron, and who had to be strongly dissuaded by Blasco from this direct action against a political opponent. Another time, while writing *Entre naranjos (Among the Orange Trees)*, his novel of passionate, idyllic love, Blasco was interrupted by a band of his disciples, armed with pistols, who asked, "Don Visent, do you think we should set fire to the city?"

Blasco's novels were becoming widely known. *The Cabin* had been reprinted in a Madrid newspaper and in book form. To celebrate the publication of *Among the Orange Trees* in 1900, a banquet of honor was held in the Retiro Park in Madrid, presided over by the eminent novelist Benito Pérez Galdós. Other honors came to Blasco along with repeated reelections to the Cortes. Success of a French translation of *The Cabin* in 1901 began the international renown that was thereafter to increase through Blasco's lifetime.

At La Malvarrosa were written *Among the Orange Trees, Sónnica la cortesana (Sónnica the Courtesan), Cañas y barro (Reeds and Mud), La catedral (The Cathedral),* and *El intruso (The Intruder)*. Impulsively, when a political trick resulted in replacing Blasco's friends on the town council with a majority of monarchists who proceeded to undo all his reforms, and when Soriano was reelected to the Cortes through the use of blackmail, the author became disheartened, and in 1904 departed to take up residence in Madrid. In a farewell speech to his followers, he said that instead of transforming Valencia into a New Athens, local tactics were degrading it into a den of cannibals, and ended with the words: "Warfare has triumphed! Hurrah for madness!" He never thereafter returned to live at La Malvarrosa. "How much time I wasted on Valencia!" he once muttered to a friend. But he had wrought greatly for his city, which is imperishably enshrined in his early novels.

CHAPTER 2

Wanderings of a Cosmopolite

ALTHOUGH Blasco was to return to Valencia several times in triumph, he left in his early thirties and thereafter lived in Madrid and other cities, traveling from time to time to places like Seville or Bilbao in search of new settings for his novels. Then his travels took him for six years to South America. After weathering World War I in Paris, he moved to the Riviera, and later took a luxury cruise around the world.

Yet through all his travels he was a partisan of the republican cause. One of his attacks published against the Spanish régime resulted in a demand that he be extradited from France for punishment. He was also in actual danger of being kidnapped and taken to Fascist Italy to be made away with. One Italian publisher with whom he had a contract issued Blasco's books with a label regretting that he was obligated to handle the works of "that anti-Fascist swine." Blasco did not live to see the day when Alfonso XIII fled into exile and the Second Republic was founded in Spain, but to his efforts was due in no small part the final overthrow of the Primo de Rivera dictatorship and the resulting ill-fated experiment in democracy.

And all through his later years, Blasco issued novel after novel, with greater and greater popular success. *The Four Horsemen of the Apocalypse* held the world's best-seller record, was translated into a dozen languages and made into a famous film, and enabled Blasco to live the life of a millionaire. *Mare Nostrum* and four other novels were also made into Hollywood pictures. Yet Blasco did not retire and rest on his earnings. He began writing a series of works that would glorify Spanish enterprise and heroism. He published several of these before his death in the Riviera mansion he had built, which in his will he left to "writers of all nations."

I *A Novelist in the New World*

Blasco and his family settled in 1904 in Madrid, where his life was divided, as usual, between politics and literature. He gave speeches in the Cortes, wrote politically devastating articles, and published a series of "social protest" novels. He lived at 8, Calle Salas, a small street in a region then suburban but now not far from the busy section of the city near the American Embassy and the Castellana Hilton Hotel. From here the author could stroll to the studios of his Valencian artist friends, the brothers Benlliure and the painter Joaquín Sorolla, who had known Blasco on the beach at La Malvarrosa and who in 1906 painted the famous portrait of him now hanging in the halls of the Hispanic Society of America in New York.

Blasco also enjoyed visiting the treasurehouse of El Prado museum and taking excursions to Toledo, the Escorial, the palace of Aranjuez, Segovia, and Ávila. He continued to indulge his love of good music and tried not to miss any concerts that included Wagner or Beethoven—the geniuses he classed at the top along with Cervantes, Goya, Victor Hugo, and Zola.

Those who accuse Blasco of ruthlessness have forgotten that in Madrid in 1907 he wrote a novel, *La voluntad de vivir (The Will to Live)*, which he suppressed because he feared it might hurt the feelings of a friend. The edition was printed and an advance copy sent to an important reviewer. When Blasco learned that the forthcoming notice would treat his work as a *roman à clef* and that the main character, Dr. Valdivia, along with others, was to be revealed as a ridiculous member of Blasco's real-life Madrid circle, he immediately ordered that the entire edition of twelve thousand copies, except for one copy, be burned, at his expense. The book was not finally published until 1953.

Once, as the result of a speech he made in the Cortes, Blasco was forced to fight another duel—this time against a monarchist lieutenant in the Security forces. The rule was that each man could fire three times. The life of the novelist was saved only when a ball partly pierced his steel belt buckle. The duel, held on the outskirts of the city, was witnessed by a gang of laborers who were building a new gas works, and who egged on the combatants by cheers and hoots. Blasco, disillusioned, remarked bitterly: "To think that these are the sort of people for whose betterment I am risking my life! I should leave these arid fields of politics, and cultivate others." [1]

His enthusiasm for the cause of social justice, however, did not falter. He continued his series of protest novels with such works as *La bodega (The Wine Cellar)* and *La horda (The Horde)*, showing the evils of poverty and slum conditions. In general, this group of novels, which had begun with *La catedral (The Cathedral)* and *El intruso (The Intruder)*, were liberal in spirit and against reaction, tradition, hypocrisy, bourgeois smugness—anything, in his opinion, standing for the monarchy, the Church, and the current economic system. Each was set mainly in a different Spanish city. Whereas the Valencian novels had been sober, pictorial, and realistic, the social novels were discursive, unobjective, and sometimes propagandistic, reflecting more strongly the author's party politics.

Blasco's life in Madrid was a busy one, devoted not merely to writing fiction. He founded the Editorial Española-Americana, which began publishing a series of "illustrated novels." Around 1913, this publishing house was to be consolidated with that of Blasco's old friend Francisco Sempere to become Editorial Prometeo of Valencia, famed in the Hispanic publishing world. The town council of Valencia agreed to give Blasco's name to the plaza formerly called La Reina. Through the influence of his old Paris friend Georges Clemenceau, then Premier of France, Blasco was named a chevalier of the Legion of Honor, later rising to the post of commander.

Blasco was elected Valencian deputy to the Cortes for the sixth time in 1907. Tiring of Madrid in August, he went to see a maritime exhibit in Bordeaux. Recalling that his doctor had advised "taking the waters" at Vichy, Blasco spent some time there. Bored, he wandered on to Geneva, Berne, Zurich, the Rhine. Then, why not go on to Munich and Salzburg, to enjoy the luxury of German music? Beyond lay Venice, and then Budapest, and finally Blasco arrived to view the Byzantine scenes of Constantinople and to meet the Sultan of Turkey.

Returning through the Balkans on the Orient Express, he found all well until at breakfast time, when Blasco was in the diner, the train collided with a local on the outskirts of Budapest. Two of the express coaches were splintered, and the author barely escaped from the wreck with his life. He returned to "civilized" Europe as a survivor, crossing the fields with his clothing over his shoulder, to get another train back home to Spain. The episode, however, made a good ending for his travel volume, *Oriente (Orient)*, 1907.

Two important novels came from his pen in 1908—*Sangre y arena (Blood and Sand)* and *Los muertos mandan (The Dead Command)*. The following year, however, he was to resign from the Cortes—although again elected—and take a step that would divert him from writing novels for some time, and involve him in the most energetic phase of his entire life.

A description of Blasco at about this time by his acquaintance Eduardo Zamacois is worth quoting:

He is tall, broad, massive. Between his eyebrows, contemplation has deeply marked its imperious vertical furrow. He is dressed in a rough cloak buckled over his herculean neck, short and plump, overflowing with vital fluids. The handclasp with which he greets me is amiable and cordial, but rough, like those exchanged by athletes before grappling in the arena. His voice is strong—a sailor's voice—his speech copious, brusque, and generously sprinkled with interjections. He looks like an artist . . . but also like a conqueror; one of those legendary adventurers who, forced to defend themselves at the same time with lance and shield, knew how to guide their mounts solely with their knees, and who, although few, sufficed to thin out the American redskins. . . . Born at the end of the fifteenth century, he would have worn armor and followed the crimson star of Pizarro or Cortés.[2]

The novelist's fame had spread widely, and he was especially appreciated in Buenos Aires, then the third largest Spanish-speaking city in the world, after Madrid and Barcelona. He accepted an invitation to visit Argentina and give a series of literary lectures. The reception by fifty thousand people at the port when his steamer, the "Cap Milano," arrived from Lisbon was one of the most enthusiastic exhibitions that the city had ever known, and he was escorted to his hotel with wild acclaim.

II   *Eclipse and Apocalypse*

It had been planned that Blasco's lectures at the Odeón would alternate with those of Anatole France; but the man from Valencia completely put the Frenchman in the shade. Anatole France stuck to his announced topic of Rabelais. But the voluble Blasco would go on for hours, talking extemporaneously on Napoleon, Wagner, the Renaissance painters, the French Revolution, Cervantes, cooking, philosophy, the contemporary theater, science, social conditions. . .

As a result of his popularity he prolonged his tour for nine months and circled Argentina, Paraguay, and Chile, giving in all about 120 lectures, to great applause. He would get from a friend a briefing on an unknown city, and with his remarkable memory and power of improvisation would expand his talk into a history of the city and a tribute to its special qualities that would flatter his listeners into mad cheers.

The trip was not, however, without its dangerous periods. When Blasco arrived at Santiago, Chile, his reputation as an atheist had aroused violent opposition and riots in the streets. Advised to return to Argentina in safety, he was indignant. "Come what may," he said, "we must face the situation. Announce at once a public meeting at which I will explain my ideas to the public of Chile who protest against me."

"Do you know what you are asking me, Don Vicente?" inquired his horrified host.

"Yes. Simply announce a lecture that I will give, and without charge!"

The crowd that gathered was hostile at first, but Blasco by now was a master at handling crowds. Despite the shrieking of the mob that overflowed the coliseum, he strode out under the candelabra, virile and energetic. Raising his arms and his voice, he began: "People of Chile, I have come here in peace. The war you have aroused against me is ignoble, unsuited to a valiant race that has not descended from Aztecs or Goths. I have come to visit you as a Spanish man of letters, a novelist, not a politician or a revolutionary.... But if I am received as an enemy, I shall not hide or flee; if again I have to smell gunpowder, I shall know how to act.... In that case I shall have to replace my announced literary lectures with others on politics and theory. I don't wish to do this.... I have come in peace..."

Little by little, the miracle of Blasco's oratory subdued the objectors. At the end of his talk, the multitude poured into the streets of the capital, wildly acclaiming the visiting celebrity who had faced them frankly.[3] By this gesture, Blasco had captured Chile, and thereafter the country was to admire him greatly and he was to marry, after the death of his first wife, a lady of a socially prominent Chilean family.

He returned to Madrid early in 1910 and began writing in the next six months a tremendous volume entitled *Argentina y sus grandezas (Argentina and Its Grandeurs)*, liberally illustrated and vividly presenting the beauties and opportunities of this large Latin-American land. His efforts on this new project so strained even his rugged constitution that he exhausted himself to the point, one day, of fainting on the street. He interrupted his promotional labors long enough to make a speech in Valencia, which cherished its favorite son more than ever. His talk on "The Novel and Its Social Influence," which held his audience for two hours and a quarter, is still remembered and quoted.

Blasco's book on Argentina was part of a new project. Now he was picturing himself as a peaceful conqueror of the New World. The government of Argentina had offered him a concession to develop several square miles along the Río Negro in midmost Patagonia, and Blasco was afire with his dream of building a city.

I felt the temptation of the primitive territories, the fever of battling against savage lands, entertaining myself with evoking in melancholy the labor of the first white men who arrived to civilize the West

Indies. . . . . The dream of becoming a millionaire, even for a season; the prospect of commanding an army of workers, to transform the aspect of a corner of the world, to build habitations in the desert, were visions so brilliant that I could not run the risk of rejecting such a gigantic enterprise.[4]

He recruited a shipload of colonists—many of them from Valencia, with experience in the art of irrigation—and went back to Argentina. In a few months he had completely transformed himself from an author into a colonizer. Blasco ascended the Andes on horseback, wrapped in a poncho; he fraternized with half-cannibal Indians; he planned a future Patagonian city with plazas, fountains, and railway station; in a fur cassock he directed the opening of irrigation canals; he supervised the operation of brickmaking; he explored the pampas, firing his rifle at strange game. The region he proposed to settle was broad, desolate, subject to cloudbursts when mirages were not rising from the Sahara-like dunes. Blasco named the future city Cervantes.

As if one quixotic colonization venture in Patagonia, with zero temperatures in winter, were not enough for this man, Blasco undertook a second one, this time in the depths of the tropics. This city, in the extreme northern Argentine province of Corrientes near the borders of Uruguay and Paraguay, facing the Gran Chaco, Blasco christened Nueva Valencia. He built a small ranch house of wood, hung on the wall a puma hide, and from there directed the starting of a quite different agricultural development.

Bearded and dirty, and wondering how his health stood the strain of traveling between extremes of tropic and freezing, Blasco would spend four days and nights on the train from Nueva Valencia to Cervantes, give his orders, and depart the same afternoon on the return journey, totaling a round trip of eight days on the train. On the banks of the Río Negro, when not huddling away from the cold, he would gallop among Patagonian sandstorms. A few nights later, bedding down at his Corrientes ranch after a fiery tropical sunset, he would listen to the rats screaming with terror as they were pursued by jungle snakes.

The worst battle for Blasco, however, was not against nature or Indians or colonizers, but against economic problems. He was a novelist, not a financier. In 1913 Argentina was struck by a heavy depression which brought financial panic, and Blasco decided that he should devote no more of his time to this South American adventure. For five years he had not touched a pen. Filled with new impressions of the glory and variety of New World scenes, the author felt that he should return to his proper métier. His interest in the town of Cervantes he sold at a loss to a colonization society. Nueva Valencia was put in the hands of a banker, and Blasco went off to Paris to write his first novel in six years. But word came that the banker had failed, and Blasco returned for the last time to Argentina early in 1914 to try and salvage what he could.

Blasco Ibáñez returned to Europe on the last German steamer that reached the continent before the outbreak of World War I. In the middle of 1914 was published *Los Argonautas (The Argonauts)*, dealing with the Atlantic Ocean and the international scene. In August the war erupted, and Blasco immediately rushed to the support of the Allies—especially the people of France, which had always been his second country. He began to write a large, illustrated *Historia de la guerra europea (History of the European War)*, printed weekly in Valencia and finally bound in nine oversize volumes. He made a tour of neutral Spain in 1915 to arouse wartime enthusiasm, and ran dangers in his country from the many German sympathizers.

Blasco's greatest contribution to the Allied cause, however, was to write the novel which became his most celebrated. In Paris in November, 1915, he began a story about a family of Europeans living on the Argentine pampas under the headship of old Madariaga, horseman and patriarch. Despite their isolation, the members of this family are drawn into the holocaust on the Western Front. He called his book *Los cuatro jinetes del Apocalipsis (The Four Horsemen of the Apocalypse)*, and its mingled romance and realism—Blasco had made trips to the front lines along the Marne to observe the war for himself—created eventually a literary earthquake.

III   *Lost: An Eagle and a Serpent*

It was almost by accident that this popular book was ever translated into English, but once it was on the market, it proved to be the story that everybody wanted to read. Within two years, two million hardbound copies of this translation had been sold, breaking all records. A few years later the *Illustrated London News* labeled it "the work which, it is said, has been the most widely read book ever printed, except for the Bible." The film rights brought $200,000. The resulting picture made a star of Rudolph Valentino; another version was screened as recently as 1962. The motion-picture appeal of Blasco's work was so great that Valentino also played the lead in *Blood and Sand;* and Blasco's next two war novels, *Mare Nostrum* and *Los enemigos de la mujer (Enemies of Women)* were eagerly seized and filmed by the Hollywood potentates.[5]

Blasco Ibáñez has so often been falsely painted as a calculating, tongue-in-cheek fabricator of vulgar best sellers which capitalized on the demand for war novels that it is worth mentioning the exact circumstances of the English publication of this epochal book, *The Four Horsemen of the Apocalypse.* The author's main intention in writing it was not greatly different from that dominating most of his other novels. He had spent six years in South America and, as part of a long-term plan of writing a series that would reveal the challenges and triumphs of European explorers and emigrants in the New World, he gave much of his opening space to family life in Argentina as a prelude to the war sections. The enthusiasm he felt for the justness of the French cause, for the *poilu* defenders of the land of Victor Hugo and the Rights of Man, was heartfelt, and the heroism of his characters was not the outcome of a tear-jerking formula. He was living in Paris on one thousand pesetas a month sent him by Editorial Prometeo in Valencia. He did not dream of the possible torrent of gold that might shower down upon him through exploitation of the book in translation, but after finishing *The Four Horsemen of the Apocalypse* immediately went on to the writing of his novel about a sea captain in the Mediterranean.

Blasco sold his entire English translation rights to Mrs. Charlotte Brewster Jordan for $300 and forgot about the deal.

Mrs. Jordan translated the novel and then began a peregrination among American publishers to find one who would take the book. No one wanted *The Four Horsemen.* The market was glutted with fine war books which the public would not buy. Mrs. Jordan finally went to E. P. Dutton and Company. The head of that firm, Mr. John Macrae, is of Scotch descent—a hard-headed businessman who, strangely enough, will, once in a while, take the most fantastic chances. . . . He took the manuscript, dropped it in his safe, and forgot it. . . . One day his printer came and asked him if he had anything to put in type because his men had nothing to do and he was afraid he could not hold them unless he kept them busy. Mr. Macrae looked into his safe and found the manuscript of *The Four Horsemen.* 'Take it and keep your men busy with it.' When the first galleys came in, the reader could not make head or tail of them. It seems that the typesetter was a man of German extraction. He didn't like the book, so he proceeded to ruin it. There was a moment when the fate of *The Four Horsemen* hung in the balance. Mr. Macrae finally decided to go ahead. It is reported that by 1924, two million copies had been sold at $1.90 each. If these figures are correct—they are probably exaggerated—the translator should have received [a royalty of] $570,000 for her work, and the author $300. As a matter of fact, the contract was later changed. Blasco Ibáñez got several thousand dollars.[6]

The book came out in the United States the week after the Armistice and headed the best-seller list for many months. It went through more than two hundred printings in this country and was translated into a dozen other languages. Although Blasco received little from royalties on his most popular book, the demand for succeeding volumes and for film rights soon made him rich. He moved to the French Riviera, at Menton, where he would be free to write and entertain in luxury. The boy born on the Street of the New Soap Factory in Valencia had come a long way.

The people of other countries wanted to see Blasco and hear him. He was especially popular in the United States, and in the fall of 1919 he accepted a lecture tour there, intending to stay about three months. As it turned out, he remained until July, 1920, including during his visit a side trip to report on the Mexican revolution. According to his later claim, he covered the United States, lecturing in Spanish almost every day, in universities, churches, moving-picture houses, and anywhere else he could entertain a crowd. Actually his schedule was not that severe, but he was a guest in the House of Representatives in Washington, spoke at West Point and at a journalists' convention in Philadelphia, and was awarded a doctoral degree *honoris causa* by George Washington University. For the *New York World* he covered the Republican Convention that nominated Warren G. Harding, at one thousand dollars for each brief despatch.

Blasco was besieged by publishers, magazine editors, and film agents. Two more movies were to be made from his books: *The Temptress* from *La tierra de todos (The Land of Everyone)*, 1921, an early role for Greta Garbo; and *The Torrent*, made from his early love story, *Among the Orange Trees*, the setting of which was changed from Valencia to Mexico. Blasco had become fascinated with the possibilities of the "seventh art" as a new way to tell stories by pictures, and felt that the film rivaled the novel in its flexibility and the rapidity with which it could change scenes and arouse conviction. His book *El paraíso de las mujeres (The Paradise of Women)*, 1922, inspired by a childhood reading of *Gulliver's Travels*, was intended as a film script. Indeed, as early as 1915, in the middle of a world war, Blasco had formed a film company to capitalize on this new medium. A group of actors went to Seville, and under his direction made a picture of *Blood and Sand*, based on a scenario by Blasco himself. The company was disbanded when a fire in the Paris studio destroyed the film and Blasco escaped a flaming death almost by a miracle.

Blasco's novels were also adapted as successful stage plays, both in Spain and in France. *Blood and Sand, The Horde,* and *Reeds and Mud* were staged in Madrid as plays of the old *zarzuela* (musical comedy) type.

Valencia had not forgotten her son, and beginning on May 15, 1921, a week-long fiesta was held in his honor. The ancient plaza of Cajeros was renamed for him. Next day he was created Honorary Director of the Centro de Cultura Valenciana, and took the occasion during his speech to suggest that the people of the city unite to erect a great museum of Valencian history that would remind everyone of their colorful past. More than one Valencian was ready to say: "I was not envious, since I appreciated the rare case that a Spaniard—moreover, a Valencian—had made himself a millionaire with his pen and was still happy to be my friend." [7]

Blasco had gone to Mexico in 1920 to get material for a novel to be called *El águila y la serpiente (The Eagle and the Serpent),* but the dispatches collected in his book *El militarismo mejicano* were so condemnatory of some of the bandits and grafters who were then running Mexico under the Carranza régime that an outcry of hatred arose against him there. Back at Menton he wrote all but three chapters of the novel; but, although he had been offered $40,000 just for the magazine rights, his indignation about the attacks upon him by some Mexicans impelled him, as an act of retaliation, to decide not to publish this novel about a Spanish-speaking country in the New World.

IV   *Do You See the Caravel?*

For several years, Blasco had been planning a series of novels that would glorify Spanish heroes, especially the bold adventurers who had built the largest empire upon which the sun had never set. The books would "show all contemporary life in the Spanish-American countries and all their hopes for the future, evoking at the same time the great epic of the conquistadores." [8] He told Dr. Balseiro: "The Spaniard is the adventurer *par excellence,* and in all corners of the earth left his traces in blood and love. I wish to do a whole group of novels on behalf of Spain and its history." [9] As in the famed series by Balzac and Zola, each book would be a separate story but together would form a cyclopean saga of the Spanish race.

Blasco had already in 1914 published a sort of prologue in *The*

Argonauts, with its Atlantic setting recalling the discovery of America, and he planned a second on Alonso de Ojeda and Vasco Núñez de Balboa, a third on the conquest of Mexico by Hernán Cortés, a fourth on Pizarro in Peru. This dream, interrupted by the war and by further travels, was now being realized. In his comfortable library at Fontana Rosa he wrote *La reina Calafia (Queen Calafia),* 1923. In it he began using a device that would tell a modern love story with a background of historical narrative, designed to lure the reader and at the same time educate him in the achievements of the Spanish people. For example, the Calafia romance, with an imperious heroine who is the modern embodiment of the fabled Amazon whose distant golden island gave its name to California, at times stops completely while a professor lectures for two chapters on the history of California from Cortés to Rezanov.

Similar methods were used in the rest of the series that Blasco completed before his death, some of which were published posthumously. *El papa del mar (The Pope of the Sea),* 1925, deals with Pedro de Luna, later Benedict XIII, first Spanish pope and last great pope of Avignon. *A los pies de Venus (At the Feet of Venus),* 1926, is a novel about the great Spanish family of Borgia. *En busca del Gran Kan (In Search of the Great Khan),* 1929, retelling the discovery of America, magnifies the deeds of the helpers of Columbus, somewhat at the expense of the traditional image of the captain of the "Santa María." *El Caballero de la Virgen (The Knight of the Virgin),* 1929, tells of Alonso de Ojeda, follower of Columbus and early explorer of Panama. *El fantasma de las alas de oro (The Phantom with Wings of Gold),* Blasco's last book, finally breaks away from the series idea and is a return to the Riviera setting.

Interrupting this outpouring of evocative adventure came another adventure of Blasco's own. He decided to make a trip around the world. Some fifty years ago, such a program did not lie within the power of everyone with a passport and a credit card. But Blasco was able to travel in company with a friendly group of wealthy celebrities on the luxury liner "Franconia." They departed from New York in October, 1923, and spent six months making the circuit, by way of Havana, Panama, the Pacific Coast, the Hawaiian Islands, Japan, China, the Philippines, Java, India, Ceylon, the Sudan, Egypt, and the Mediterranean. With the skilled pen and shrewd eye of a novelist, Blasco produced a series of articles, for each of which Hearst's *International Magazine* paid him a thousand dollars. These were collected and published in Spanish in three volumes in 1924–1925 and in English the following year as *A Novelist's Tour of the World.* Of it he wrote in a letter of June 18, 1924: "I think it will be my best work; the one that will be read longest after my death."

Blasco wrote short stories all his life, and back on the Riviera finished the last of six volumes of such stories, for which he was paid top prices. He boasted that he could make a thousand dollars turning out a tale in an afternoon. The shower of riches that had fallen upon the former shopkeeper's son naturally changed his way of living, and he was now driving a Cadillac and talking about buying a yacht, which he proposed to present to a friend when he got tired of it.

But despite his vaunted wealth and his interest in building the palace at Fontana Rosa, he still kept up an active part in politics-in-exile. In 1923 the coup d'état of Primo de Rivera aroused widespread alarm, and a campaign of continued pressure against the monarchy was planned. For his part, Blasco in 1924 wrote a polemic volume entitled *Alfonso XIII desenmascarado (Alfonso XIII Unmasked)*. The attack was so violent that the Spanish government demanded Blasco's extradition, but it was not granted and other worries came to distract Alfonso and Dictator Primo de Rivera. The following April, Blasco wrote in Paris a manifesto, "What the Spanish Republic Should Be," which was widely circulated clandestinely. But his enemies were ideas, not people. One of his best friends on the Riviera was Don Jaime de Borbón, pretender to the Spanish throne!

Blasco's wife María died in January, 1925, and was buried with marked expressions of mourning. His second wife, whom he married in October, was Elena Ortúzar Bulnes, daughter of a noted Chilean general—a lady whom he affectionally called "Chita." She lived until 1965 and died in her native country. She helped him take care of his health—now an important consideration. Blasco was sixty, but he refused the offer of his friend Dr. Sergei Voronoff to submit to a rejuvenating operation, saying that he fully expected to live to be eighty. But his eyesight was becoming badly affected, to the point where he traveled to Switzerland and Paris to obtain relief. In France, he came down with grippe. Moreover, diabetes, which he had inherited from his father, was becoming acute, and insulin was not yet widely used to alleviate this affliction.

Blasco returned to his beloved Fontana Rosa and continued to work. He was now embarking on a big book about the League of Nations and the future peace of the world, to be called *The Fifth Horseman of the Apocalypse*. At a time when others were beginning to think of death, Blasco was thinking as usual of the future. He believed his body was as vigorous as his spirit. He planned fresh travels—back to the United

States, to Chile, to the Andes. He would take another trip around the world . . .

It was January 28, 1928, the eve of his sixty-first birthday. At two o'clock in the morning he called his secretary and tried to dictate the opening paragraph of his new book; but he was suffering from bronchial pneumonia and could barely breathe. His mind soon wandered, and he began to talk of plans for extending his beloved garden at Fontana Rosa, outside the window. (His will provided that this entire estate, on the death of his second wife, would be a gift to "all the writers of the world.") "I wish," he said, "that the garden resemble those of Valencia, my Valencia. . . ." Then he thought how, a few days before, he had shown a model of a Spanish caravel to the man who was doing the illustrations for the Columbus novel. "Do you see the caravel?" he rambled. "I see it now—with its sails bellying to the wind."

When the final moment came, before dawn, Don Vicente thought he saw the approach of his spiritual godfather, and exclaimed: "It's Victor Hugo . . . Victor Hugo. . . . Let him come in!" His head fell on his wife's shoulder and the final words came: "My garden! My garden!"

Blasco Ibáñez had cultivated his garden, but he had also been one of the forerunners of the Second Spanish Republic, proclaimed on April 14, 1931—in the defense of which many an American died between 1936 and 1939. He wished to be buried in France, but in 1933 his body, carried by ship to Valencia, was greeted at the dock by a cheering mass of his fellow townsmen, and was buried with full military honors in the Civil Cemetery, a few miles inland from the beach and the old part of the city where the novelist was born. The city council which had once served and then flouted him now issued a booklet to commemorate the great return, and quoted eight pages of encomiums from literary critics.

Although the capture of Valencia by Franco's troops in 1939 resulted in the attempted destruction of every trace of the existence of this prophet of the Republic, there still remains in Valencia and in Spain a memory of the sixteen-year-old boy who was sentenced to six months in prison for writing a poem. No streets or squares in all of Spain are named for Vicente Blasco Ibáñez. But in a thousand Spanish bookshops his volumes, from *Rice and a Carriage* to *The Phantom with Wings of Gold,* are to be seen in the show windows. His books are famed, too, in many other parts of the world; next to Cervantes, he is the Spanish author most frequently translated. And in whatever language he is read, the author of *The Cabin* and *The Mayflower* will not soon be forgotten.

CHAPTER 3

The Early Valencian Novels

M OST authors write best about what they know best. This was especially true of Blasco Ibáñez; there is always a close connection between where he is writing and what he is writing about. He began by cultivating his own garden—the beautiful but violent garden of the province of Valencia, with its sun and scenery and its vivid history, for centuries tinged with Arabic culture as well as Christian. The result was a group of six novels and two volumes of short stories which have forever preserved the region as nobody else has done; in fact, one suspects that no other Spanish novelist has presented his homeplace in literature with such completeness.[1]

Regional realism needs no defense, for some of the greatest novelists are remembered for starting from a particular base and expanding their local but unparochial observations into reflections of the universal. To quote Seneca (a Spaniard): *Nusquam est qui ubique est* ("He who is everywhere is nowhere"). Reading many of the Valencian pages of Blasco, one also gets the feeling that here the countryside has found its own voice and is speaking through his pen.

The Valencian group comprises *Arroz y tartana (Rice and a Carriage)*, 1894, dealing with the city and particularly its bourgeois group of status-seekers; *Flor de mayo (The Mayflower)*, 1896, picturing the waterfront, the fisherfolk, and the sea; *La barraca (The Cabin)*, 1898, a masterpiece of peasant life in the environs of the city; *Entre naranjos (Among the Orange Trees)*, 1900, with its setting in a small town in the heart of the citrus orchards; *Sónnica la cortesana (Sónnica the Courtesan)*, 1901, presenting the most memorable episode in Valencia's history, the siege of Sagunto (the Spanish form of the Latin "Saguntum") by Hannibal; and *Cañas y barro (Reeds and Mud)*, 1902, depicting the lives of the people of La Albufera, the great lake to the south of the city. All but the last of these volumes were first published as serials in *El Pueblo*, Blasco's republican daily newspaper. He also presented Valencia in his first two volumes of short stories: *Cuentos valencianos (Valencian Stories),* 1896, and *La condenada (The Condemned Woman),* 1900; these will be discussed in Chapter 9.

I *The Naturalistic Trap is Sprung*

The almost intolerable conditions under which these works were written are described in Blasco's foreword to *The Mayflower:* "at dawn, in the shabby editorial office of a newspaper as yet of uncertain survival, the author, lulled by the pounding of the press that revolved on the ground floor, turning out the first copies of the paper, and hearing the thousand sounds of a city awakening to live another day. My work as a novelist would continue until one more day was well along or else until physical fatigue and an unwelcome drowsiness began to overcome me" (I, 395–96).[2] But by 1898 his work was nationally known, and by 1900 with *Among the Orange Trees* he was given homage as a writer in the forefront of Spanish novelists. The universal acclaim of the Valencian group merits a closer attention than will be given to his later works, and hence in the present and following chapter more specific analysis will be offered than space permits for most of the later Blasco books.

The "Valencian group" is almost always discussed as if the eight books were a planned series comparable to Balzac's *Cómedie Humaine* or Zola's studies of milieu, following the fortunes of a family or "handling" a particular trade or class. Actually, the only thing that these early outpourings of Blasco's genius have in common is that all the settings are in or near the city of Valencia. In style, characterization, theme, and action, they differ greatly from one to another. They all share, however, the author's "descriptionist mania," as one writer termed his frequent rendering of familiar scenes, using the appeals to all the senses which earned him also labels like "colorist," "impressionist," and "landscape painter."[3] He has been associated with the Valencian group of artists such as Joaquín Sorolla and the brothers Benlliuret, whose daring use of color and sheen shocked the *fin-de-siècle* conservatives.

These scenes that Blasco described were, however, daily before his eyes. Almost all were drawn from his own life. Of all the six novels, only *Sónnica* was researched; for the material of the others, all the young novelist had to do was to open his photographic eyes to the life around him, or at most to take excursions north as far as Cape Bagur or south to the port of Algiers.

A common quality among the novels and stories is the frequent recourse to violent action that at times verges on melodrama. Underneath the levantine placidity and fatalism lies a smouldering scoria which often erupts when repression becomes unbearable.[4] The only other marked quality found in all these novels except *The Cabin* is the succumbing of a young man to the dominance or mortal power of a woman. This pattern, found also in later novels, is prominent in the very first of Blasco's "serious" novels, *Rice and a Carriage.*

This early effort was the only one admittedly written under the influence of Zola. It does have the virtues and defects of the naturalist equation, in which character is the sum of heredity plus environment. The environment of the city of Valencia around 1890 is shown to influence the characters by making misers, spendthrifts, or fools even of those persons who inherited a tough Aragonese temperament.

The title of *Rice and a Carriage* suggests clearly the theme. It is drawn from the quoted first verse of a popular song that might be translated:

> Rice and a carriage,
> Modish all the while—
> And let the ball whirl
> In Valencian style!

This expression ridicules the *petite bourgeoisie* that attempts to dazzle the public by vain show. To ride in a carriage, even though the family must live behind the walls of their home on the cheapest of foods, is the symbol that is supposed to overwhelm the humble classes plodding in the dust. One might borrow, beg, or gamble, or go to the most vicious lengths in order to maintain this appearance. Blasco, who himself came from the shopkeeping class, perfectly portrays this feckless group that, "held in the middle of its social metamorphosis, has one foot among the common people, from which it comes, and the other among the aristocracy, toward which it aims" (I, 361). Inevitably, the strain of keeping up with the grandees will lead to sorrow.

The ending is thus predestined, but the story is deftly handled, and the reader soon gets acquainted with the fairly large cast of characters. They center around a prosperous dry-goods shop, Las Tres Rosas (The Three Roses), founded in 1832 by Don Eugenio García, who had been abandoned in the marketplace as a child by his poor Aragonese parents. But the main characters are Juan and Manuela Fora, offspring of a family once wealthy from the silk-weaving business before that Valencian industry had been ruined by the cheap goods of Lyons in France.

The novel opens with Doña Manuela, twice widowed but still a fine figure of a woman at fifty. In her youth she had loved a scapegrace cousin, Rafael Pajares, but in a fit of pique had married Melchor Peña, chief clerk at Las Tres Rosas, who had become wealthy as owner of the business. Their only son, Juanito, takes after his father and happily works in the shop, turning over all his wages to his mother, whom he idolizes just this side of madness. After Melchor, who had lavished his earnings to keep up his wife's aspirations, died—apparently from the strain of social climbing—Manuela married her old flame, Rafael, and their three children were reared in luxury while their father spent Manuela's inheritance in wild extravagance before his death. Extravagance, however, is also Manuela's vice, and during the seven months in which the action of the novel takes place, she sinks more and more deeply into degradation.

Her chief victim is her son Juanito, now aged thirty and bearded, but still childlike in his innocence. He co-signs his mother's borrowings, and in desperation sells his property and plunges into the stock market, joining the mania of the moment in which people like Antonio Cuadros, now manager of Las Tres Rosas, are led to gamble insanely. Juanito even causes his seamstress sweetheart and her duenna to put all their savings into the hands of Ramón Morte, seemingly a benevolent broker who is sure the market will rise.

A crisis comes when the family horse dies and the Pajares family, in all their finery (still unpaid for), must appear on the Alameda on foot, feeling themselves disdained by all their carriage-riding peers. In order to obtain money for another horse, Doña Manuela stoops so low as to accept the "protection" of Cuadros, a former clerk who had married her maidservant but who now was rich from his dealings on the exchange. Despite all the warnings of her brother, who has refused to encourage her spendthrift passion by lending her anything from his hoard, she heads toward inevitable misery.

The climax comes when Juanito, outside his mother's bedroom, suffers a terrible shock when he learns of her turpitude. He wanders for hours, contemplating suicide and observing the blackness of life. When he returns, the final news comes from Madrid; the market has crashed and everyone is penniless. Juanito falls to the floor, mortally ill, destroyed by the loss of illusion, crying out: "Don't touch me, mother!" His uncle, Juan, blames Manuela for her son's lingering death.

A fitting epilogue comes when old Don Eugenio, whose savings had been taken away by Cuadros when he decamped after the debacle, observes the ruin of his proud shop. As he had prophesied, he falls dead in the square where as a child he had been deserted by his peasant parents seventy years before. "His fall was instantaneous.... Those who flocked from all the shops were able, though, to witness the death of the last veteran of the marketplace" (I, 394). The trap is sprung; the meanness of life has come full circle.

II   A Smuggler's Voyage to Algiers

Rice and a Carriage is the finest of Blasco's novels from the standpoint of presenting a picture of the milieu he knew best. If, as Zola believed, environment is extremely important, then it is extremely important for the Zolaesque-type novelist to render the environment in fully-wrought detail. Here is a superb example of the novel of *costumbrismo* or local color. Much of the detail came from Blasco's early life. For example, the crooked financier Morte was based on a real person who wrought ruin among many trusting people in Valencia before absconding in 1882. The description of the *fallas* celebration in Chapter 4 was taken from notes made in 1890 by Blasco from the balcony of his family's house at 5, Plaza de San Gil, a block from the main marketplace, to which they had moved in 1871. The structure of the book, in fact, is neatly based on the cycle of public celebrations in Valencia, starting on Christmas Eve and running through the wild *fiesta de toros* of July.

Successively, the chapters cover not only Christmas, but New Year's Day and its formal visits; carnival and Lent; the *fallas,* unique festival of Valencia on the day of St. Joseph on March 19, but going back to Moorish days of fire worship and saturnalia; the three days of Easter spent in the country villa of Burjasot, where young Vicente had written his first "novel"; the day of St. Vincent, patron of Valencia; a Sunday in spring, with lovers wandering hand in hand; the processions of Corpus Christi and the holy pageants on carts, reminiscent of similar mystery cycles in England and elsewhere; and the garish Feria de Julio, with its fireworks, bullfights, and glittering crowds that contrast violently with Juanito's mood of despair for the human race. Actually, each chapter manages to combine a genre description of a celebration with a strong turn of plot.

This novel lacks the "documentation" of the Zola school; but in its own way it is documented with Blasco's overwhelming recall of his own young manhood.[5] Some scenes, clearly, are digressions, put in for their value as local color, such as the obsequious New Year's visit of the tenant peasants or the delights of a dinner during which the young ladies have to retire and loosen their corsets to accommodate the dainty dishes still to come. But study shows that quite often the setting of a chapter is more than a bit of scene painting; the background frequently adds irony to the action.

Few details of clothing or custom, of menu or mode, escape the recollection of this son of the city. Here, as if preserved forever under a crystal bell, is the social history of Blasco's Valencia, with a thousand details significant for those who have visited that city or dream some day of going there. The novel has immoralized a city that some day, it is hoped, may again dare to give honor to its most famous citizen. It was for this quality that one early critic, González Blanco, termed Blasco "a Velásquez of literature." [6]

The structure of this novel is not only cyclical, but has been likened to that of a classic symphony; González Blanco gives several pages to this idea, and reminds the reader that Blasco had once been music critic for a Valencian newspaper.

The tone of *Rice and a Carriage* is not completely of the school of Zola. It is a shifting mixture of irony and sentiment. It is fairly objective, even though semiautobiographical; one can detect, in some passages describing Juanito, the rebellious, alienated, and lonely Vicente of his youth; and in the jealous musings of Andresito, son of the Cuadros couple and admirer of one of the two Pajares daughters, one hears the "poet" that the young Blasco used to be. In this first novel, although it appeared as a serial in a revolutionary newspaper, politics and partisanship are quite rigidly excluded; even if after the *fallas* the crowd sings the "Marseillaise" and shouts *"Viva la República,"* this could be a touch of realism from observation. Most readers could not tell from this novel whether the author was a heretic or the most devout Catholic.

The defects of the novel stem from the theories of Zola and Flaubert, the masters of naturalism. Cuadros the gambler voices a crude Darwinism when he says that the stock exchange is a fight for existence and "in order that some may live, they must devour others" (I, 339). But on the whole the book arouses not pessimism, but a detached compassion.

The main lack in the story is clear motivation. We are told that Uncle Juan is a miser and his sister Manuela is a mad waster, but we are not shown clearly why one is the opposite of the other, and we really never get into their minds. Why is Manuela such a bad mother? Nor can we believe that Juanito could live for thirty years in such childish innocence, such unawareness of his mother's mania, and then die of a brain fever that is more like an Oedipal broken heart. It may be that

Manuela is supposed to be a Spanish Madame Bovary. It is more likely
that she is a Sophia Baines, and that *Rice and a Carriage* is Blasco's
version of Arnold Bennett's *Old Wives' Tale.*[7]

Rice and a Carriage is more prodigal of good qualities, wrote
González Blanco in 1909, than any other Blasco novel. "Taken all in
all, and as a lyrical work, *Arroz y tartana* is excelled by almost all the
later ones; but in wealth of details as a work of documentation it is
perhaps unique, and he keeps in mind, as a shopworn classicist would
say, that documenting must be the supreme ideal of the consummate
writer of naturalism." And he concludes: "Never, perhaps, did Blasco
later reach this integrity and intensity of artistic sensation, in no way
deformed by anything extraneous; he was to be more pithy, more
forceful, more vigorous; but never so placid, so provincialist, in the
novel ... a lovely and clear novel resembling a great lyrico-elegiac
poem!"[8] To represent the Spanish school of *costumbrismo* or local
color, *Rice and a Carriage* is Blasco's most important work.

For his second novel to appear as a serial in *El Pueblo,* Blasco wisely
chose as a model Victor Hugo rather than Zola. Heredity and
environment still strongly mold the destinies of the characters in *Flor
de mayo (The Mayflower),* but life is tragic rather than mean, and the
protagonist emerges as the first of Blasco's strong, simple, honorable,
breadwinning heroes. "El Retor" is a classic toiler of the sea, and the
Valencian waterfront and the deeps of the Mediterranean on which the
fishermen live and die furnish settings that the author knew at first
hand. He himself lived in La Cabañal, suburb near El Grao, the port of
the city, and from boyhood had observed the fishing craft, with their
lateen sails furled, being hauled up on the beach by teams of oxen. He
went to the trouble of making a voyage to Algiers in 1895 on a
smuggling vessel in order to obtain details for a chapter, and drew also
upon a personal adventure when he was marooned during a storm on a
small island in the vast gulf of Valencia.

III   *Death and the Price of Fish*

In a valuable foreword, Blasco describes the almost impossible conditions under which four Valencian novels were written. It is amazing
that *The Mayflower* achieved unity while being written, a few pages at
a time, at dawn after a long editorial day. The book is not greatly
expanded with digressions or subplots. It is as simple and profound as
the sea itself and the people who daily risk their lives so that citizens
may enjoy a fish dinner.

In his foreword Blasco also pays tribute to a fellow artist—

a painter—whom he knew as a boy and often met later on the beach while both were studying their model: the Mediterranean Sea. This other Valencian, working in the open air, magically reproducing on his canvas the golden sunshine, the emptiness of the sky, the shifting blue of the sea, the shaggy oxen wading in the waves, the gleam of Levantine sunlight on a bather's skin—this artist was Joaquín Sorolla, lifelong friend of Blasco. Both learned their lessons well, and Blasco has been called a Sorolla who painted in words. His style does have, in *The Mayflower* and other novels, the bold, almost unbearable use of dazzling color and glare in his scene descriptions.

The Mayflower begins with one of those descriptions, the awakening of the waterfront and the assembling at daybreak of the women who sell "the fruit of the sea" in the city market. There an open battle breaks out between two sisters-in-law, who literally use the language and the weapons of fishwives, and who are not easily reconciled by the ancient matriarch of the place, Tía Picores.

The husbands of the combatants are Pascual (nicknamed El Retor, or The Curate, because of his resemblance to a well-fed cleric) and his younger brother Tonet, a dandy and spendthrift. Their father, the leading fisherman of La Cabañal, had been caught in a storm and his proud vessel tossed on the beach, a broken coffin for his drowned body. The widow, to survive, had cleverly converted the hull into a tavern for the fishing folk, and in their room in the prow the two boys had been sheltered. El Retor early goes to sea as an apprentice, but Tonet, his opposite, lives only for drink, women, and dashing clothing for which he cannot pay. Service by Tonet in the Navy makes him a better seaman but not a better man.

One of the most intense episodes is a smuggling trip to Algiers in a rickety old bark, almost as seaworthy as "an old guitar," which, if captured by the coast guard, will not bring a great loss to the backers. The brothers work together to overload the hold and deck of the cranky craft with bales of contraband tobacco. Forewarned by a spy in Algiers, the coast guard pursues the old vessel—which ironically bears the name of "Garbosa," meaning "sprightly" or "graceful"—but El Retor escapes by hiding his bark among some islands and the next night rams her ashore, where she is successfully unloaded by the smugglers.

El Retor spends the profits from this bit of business on the building of the finest fishing vessel ever seen in La Cabañal. It is named "Flor de Mayo," after the brand of tobacco which had been the cargo of the "Garbosa" (the untutored family was not aware that another *May-flower* was known to history as the bearer of the Pilgrims to New England).

The new fishing boat returns from its maiden trip heavily laden with fish caught with a seine dragged between it and a companion vessel. Tonet had not been along, for his hand, apparently wounded in a tavern fight, was bandaged. But on the eve of the second sailing, Tonet's neglected wife reveals to El Retor that for years he has been cuckolded by his brother, and that his eight-year-old son is really his nephew. The shock of the revelation and the night-long wanderings of El Retor, his refusal to catch the guilty couple and avenge the injury in hot blood, his doubts and arguments, are analyzed by the author.

For suspense and vivid description, however, Blasco never excelled the final chapter of *The Mayflower.* In the face of a storm which turns out to be the worst tempest in the memory of the oldest seaman of La Cabañal, El Retor madly puts to sea, followed by many other fishing craft. Aboard with others of the crew of the "Flor de Mayo" are the captain, who now knows himself to be the most notorious cuckold of the port; his brother Tonet, whom he had always protected but now hated; and the little son Pascualet, proud apprentice whom El Retor had dreamed of making a great fisherman and his wealthy heir.

It would be unfair to those who have never read *The Mayflower* to reveal in detail the successive events of this final chapter. The storm strikes, and El Retor is at the helm of his beautiful vessel. His unsophisticated mind torn by recollections and fears, he must make decision after decision. But the sea is violent, and the lives of those who follow it are violent as well. It is enough to say that the brothers suffer the fate of their father and life comes full circle. "The only truth was death, which never fails nor cheats," El Retor realizes as his dismasted ship is driven hopelessly toward the rocks. "And likewise the truth was the fierce hypocrisy of the sea, which lies humbly calm, which lets itself be exploited by the fishermen, which cajoles them, making them believe in its eternal goodness, and then, at a stroke, one day or another, goes on destroying them, generation after generation" (I, 476–77). The women of the family, gazing helplessly from the end of the breakwater, are overcome by the results of their acts. But the old fishwife, Tía Picores, shakes her fist at the city and curses all landsmen. "So you think the price of fish is high?" she demands. It is the same note on which ends Blasco's masterpiece *The Cabin,* written three years later: "Bread! How much it costs to win it!"

IV   *A Masterpiece about Intolerance*

Characterization is not complex in *The Mayflower,* for these are people with uncomplicated motives. But the story is enriched by sketches of half a dozen minor figures, such as Tío Paella, drunken cabdriver and father of El Retor's faithless wife; Siñor Martínez, the policeman who makes his headquarters at the tavern on the beach and departs leaving the hostess, El Retor's mother, to bear a golden-haired baby; and the old cousin of El Retor, nicknamed "El Callao" because of his daily mention of his naval service in the Pacific in 1865. Callao, of course, is the port for the Peruvian city of Lima.

The finest aspect of *The Mayflower*, however, as in *Rice and a Carriage*, is the rendering of a milieu—the fishing village and the lives of the Mediterranean seamen. Once again the celebrations of the people are lovingly described. The Holy Week procession of El Encuentro in Chapter V is unconnected with the plot, although to be sure El Retor is hereditary captain of *los judíos*, one of the two factions that confront each other. More justifiable is the careful description of the ceremony of blessing a virgin ship before "Flor de Mayo" is launched.

In this novel, once and for all, the author has enshrined this region and these folk in literature, and thereafter one who knows Blasco Ibáñez cannot think of the Valencian waterfront without being reminded of him. It is not to be wondered that, in honor of this novel, the people of the city changed the name of the street on which Blasco was born and rechristened it "Flor de Mayo."

The novel abounds in other fine descriptions. On the smuggling voyage the "Garbosa" is becalmed, and from its deck the crew could gaze into the profundities of the tranquil sea.

The clouds and the bark itself were reflected in the blue deeps like a mysterious mirage. Schools of fish wriggled, nervous and quick, brilliant as strips of tin; enormous dolphins played like frolicsome children, protruding above the surface their grotesque snouts and black backs, tinted with shiny powder; flying fish flitted away, butterflies of the sea, sinking in the mysterious depths after a few instants of life in the air; and all these strange beings, of fantastic shapes, of indefinable colors, some daubed like tigers, others black and funereal, large and robust, small and darting, with enormous mouths and small bodies or with small heads and swollen bellies, bustled and fluttered around the old vessel, as if it were one of those mythological barges in which were escorted the divinities of the sea. (I, 433)

Not only descriptive power, but subtle irony is found in Blasco's portrayal of the first sailing of the fishing fleet—a hundred craft, pair by pair for seine hauling, handled by a thousand men of the port. An ancient superstition is duly observed at the end of the breakwater.

Stay-at-homes shout out to the seamen that they are leaving their women behind to betray them. When El Retor hears himself called "cuckold," he innocently, ignorant of his disgrace, taunts his tormenters by urging them to add something more to their insults. One, provoked, replies: "Your brother Tonet is staying behind to console Dolores!" El Retor grumbles that observing the old custom of bandying insults about is all very well, but that to get personal about the family is not quite decent.

As a sample judgment on *The Mayflower,* one may quote Gerald Brenan, an English critic who does not admire the later works of Blasco, but who says of this early achievement: "Here we have the real Blasco Ibáñez, sure of his subject and his style. . . . As one reads it, the smell and glitter of the southern sea seem to rise out of its pages and to throw a cloak of poverty over the barefooted fishermen who wring a precarious living out of it. . . . Since the *Odyssey* and the *Aeneid,* I do not think that the life of the seafaring people of the Mediterranean has ever been presented so vividly." [9]

La baraca (The Cabin), third of Blasco's Valencian novels, became his first universally acclaimed masterwork, to the point that, no matter what he was later to publish, his epithet among lazy critics remained "the illustrious author of *La barraca.*" As a lesson in the casual way in which such a classic could be written, overlooked, and then discovered by the world, its early history is of much interest.

Around the middle of 1895, Blasco was sought by the police as the instigator of riots in favor of Cuban independence. He hid out for a time, while waiting to be smuggled aboard a ship bound for Italy. Four days were spent in an upstairs room in a waterfront tavern run by a young republican. With nothing to do to pass the time, Blasco borrowed from the family a bottle of violet ink, a pen, and some pads of blue-lined paper on which he wrote a story of violence among the villagers living in the Huerta, or truck-garden area on the outskirts of Valencia. When he had to escape hurriedly, all his possessions were left behind.

After his return to Spain he spent many months in prison and on parole, until election by the people of Valencia brought him immunity from further arrests. One day, while electioneering, he was greeted by the young tavernkeeper and invited to visit his old hideout, where all his things were returned to him—including the faded manuscript that Blasco read as if it were the work of another. This reading inspired him to reshape the tale in the form of a short novel that he could run as a serial in *El Pueblo.* Thus the masterpiece was created dawn after dawn, after a hard night of writing and putting together a lively newspaper. It ran in the columns of the journal without receiving much comment, and an edition of seven hundred copies was printed, of which only five hundred were sold, at a price of one peseta each. Blasco and his printer friend Sempere shared between them a profit of seventy-eight pesetas, and the book was apparently forgotten.

One day Blasco got a letter from a French teacher at a school in Bayonne who, while waiting at the station in San Sebastián, happened to pick up *The Cabin* and wished to translate it. Blasco, busy at many things, neglected to answer this letter and the three or four that followed, but finally got around to sending a note authorizing the translation, and forgot about it. Then he read in the Madrid newspapers that a novel by the Spanish deputy Blasco had appeared in Paris with enormous success, acclaimed by the foremost critics.

The author was belatedly honored in his own country. *El Liberal,* Madrid daily, ran it as a serial. The book was translated into many European languages and pirated in America, and soon sold more than a million copies.

The Cabin, which might so easily have been lost in the publishing shuffle after rewarding the author with thirty-nine pesetas, well deserves all the applause showered upon it. The final version was written in the autumn of 1898—the most critical year of the century for Spain, when loss of its last overseas possessions aroused a few thinkers to plan a better future for the country, torn by prejudice and dissension. Although Blasco did not intend it as a parable, the theme of the book might well have struck many Spanish readers as a condemnation of blind animosity among neighbors and a presage that through hard labor and hope, the strangling hand of the past might finally allow decent men at least to survive, labor harder, and continue to hope. That theme is even more pertinent today, when all men are neighbors but intolerance rages in the streets.

V *An Art That is Sure and Faultless*

Thus, in the same year that Spain lost her empire, she gained the masterpiece of one of the world's great novelists of regionalism. The theme does confirm the conviction of Blasco, man of action, that there are other men in the world who will stubbornly continue to fight for their right to live and support their families, and if need be, to outface an entire village bent upon ostracism and revenge. Batiste, the strong peasant, when hatred has destroyed everything he has in the world, can only ponder stoically: "Bread! How much it costs to win it! And how much evil it brings to mankind!" All he can do is to flee this cursed spot and begin another life, another battle to escape the talons of hunger.

The story has the simplicity of genius, and lacks any secondary plot or distraction from the progress toward the final tragedy. The *barraca* is a small, thatched farmhouse like those surrounding it in the village of Alboraya, a garden region just north of Valencia and not far from the sea. (This is a real village, with no other claim to prominence than to have served as setting for the novel.) The homestead had been the pride of the farmer called Uncle Barret, because as he worked in his fields he always wore a beret pulled down over his ears. Despite his labors he fell into the clutches of a usurious landlord, who evicted him from the land and who was then murdered by Uncle Barret in a fit of anger. For ten years the tract of land has been kept in a state of ruin by the villagers, in revenge for the fate of Barret and his family and in hatred of his heirs. Anyone who tried to take occupancy was soon scared away, and the dilapidated cabin remained a warning to landlords that the tenants could not be imposed upon too far.

One day Batiste, a man who is not easily frightened, arrives to take up occupancy. The news is spread by Pimentó, loafer and bully who constitutes himself the spearhead of the neighborhood's animosity. But despite this force, Batiste and his wife and five children labor to restore their shack and its plot of land to its former prosperous state. Dismissing the warnings of a mysterious old shepherd who claims that the land is accursed, they ignore the ostracism of every neighbor.

When threats fail, Batiste is haled before the Tribunal de las Aguas, a medieval survival which is the only court governing the use of irrigation waters in the vast Huerta of Valencia.[10] Pimentó, the local warden, accuses Batiste on three false charges. Inarticulate and friendless, angered by obvious lies, Batiste loses his temper and is heavily fined for his outburst. He is also enjoined from using the precious waters of the canals; but when he sees his plants dying, he and his family go out at night and defiantly bring water to the crop that is their only hope of sustenance.

The young girl Roseta gets work in the silk factory, and shyly begins meeting the butcher's apprentice. But one Sunday at the well, she is mocked by other girls; a fight results, the romance is revealed, and the lovers are separated forever. The three small boys go to the village school even though they have to fight their way home through a gang of students influenced by the evil words of their parents. After one fight the five-year-old child, an angelic being who, his mother predicts, is destined to be an abbot, is thrown into a slimy irrigation canal. He gets a fever from which he lies desperately ill. The other two boys stay home and with their elder brother help run the farm.

Their old horse dies, and Batiste purchases a new one at the fair in the streambed of the River Turia in the city. The first day on which the new animal is used for plowing, a cry of alarm comes from the cabin. The little boy is dying! And when Batiste finally comes back to unharness the horse, he finds that an enemy, undoubtedly Pimentó, has stabbed it in the hope of killing this prized, essential beast.

Now that things look blackest, Blasco with artistry achieves a reversal, a swing from depth to height. The death of the little one has brought a shock of remorse to the entire village. No one had spoken to the family for six months; now all the gossips and busybodies enter the *barraca* as if it were their own home, and take charge of the last rites and funeral arrangements. Pepeta, wife of Pimentó, assumes the lead, putting a horrible assemblage of flowers upon the dead child's head and painting his cheeks before he is carried off with high ceremony to the burial plot. Pimentó, with a twinge of conscience, hires a band of five musicians to accompany the parade, and the pitiful child is the center of a macabre festival that marches to the strains of a tuneless waltz played by trumpet, clarinet, and wheezy trombone.

There is hope that perhaps the family of Batiste will now be allowed to live in peace. Ostracism, however, still continues. On the day of St. John, Batiste, with money from a good harvest stored in his cabin loft, decides to relax for the first time. He has never entered the local tavern before, but is drawn to watch a drinking bout between Pimentó and two of his gang, and to accept a cup of brandy. Pimentó boasts that he had not paid his rent for years because he had terrified his landlady with stories of the fate of Barret's victim. Now, however, the game has been spoiled by the success of Batiste in breaking the boycott. Enraged, Pimentó throws a stool at the bystanding Batiste, who strikes the enemy down with it and walks out of the tavern through the muttering crowd. From now on, the village is on the side of Pimentó as a martyr to their cause, although they had often cursed him for a drunken lout. There is no appealing to the Civil Guard on such a village matter. Batiste knows that he must defend himself against Valencian vengeance or give up his homestead, where a new crop has just been planted.

Returning home in the dark one evening after shooting birds, he is fired upon from ambush and wounded in the back. He returns the shots, but the skulker, wounded in return, gets away. It is Pimentó, who throughout has embodied all the prejudice and provincial ignorance of the village. On the night when Pimentó succumbs to his wounds, Batiste lies in bed, haunted by evil dreams. Perhaps the outcome is inevitable; perhaps the *barraca* is truly built on accursed land.[11] He awakens to find his cabin on fire.

The village has taken its revenge. Not one person comes to the aid of the family. "They were more alone than in the middle of a desert; the isolation of hatred was a thousand times worse than that of Nature." And the book ends with melancholy stoicism: "And all of them, with oriental resignation, sat on the sloping bank, awaiting the dawn, with their backs aching with cold, their chests toasted by the brazier that tinged their faces with a bloody dye, observing with the passivity of fatalism the course of the fire, which was devouring all their possessions and transforming them into cinders as fragile and worthless as their earlier illusions of peace and labor." Here is naturalism that closely approaches classical tragedy.

For a final opinion on the high merit of *The Cabin*, one cannot do better than again to quote Gerald Brenan: "In every respect it is a masterpiece. Its plot has the firmness and cleanness of the plot of a Maupassant story and yet it has been able to take up and digest all the innumerable details required to convey the life of a peasant community. From the very beautiful opening, with its description of day breaking over the Vega and the work of the farms beginning, to the terrific scene of the burning homestead and the stampede of the scorched animals that closes the book, it moves with an art that is sure and faultless. And as a picture of peasant life it is unequalled, I think, in any language." [12]

CHAPTER 4

The Later Valencian Novels

BLASCO'S novels about his home province continued to be issued without interruption into the twentieth century. His next book, written in the autumn of 1900, was his most passionate love story, reminiscent of the romances of Gabriele D'Annunzio. The setting of *Entre naranjos (Among the Orange Trees)* is the town of Alcira, in the Huerta, with its square miles of orange groves south of the Albufera and the city of Valencia. This region was quite familiar to Blasco, who had made frequent electoral excursions to such provincial places and observed the narrow conventionality of the orange barons.

The material lay before his eyes, and possibly in his biography and his heart. He used not only the beauties and economics of the rich Huerta, but also the routines and boredom of his service in the National Congress, of which he had been a member for two years. And the love affair in the book probably derived from Blasco's own life. "It has the added attraction of certain autobiographical details," says Eduardo Zamacois. "The interesting figure of Leonora Moreno might well have been a Russian artiste very well known to the author." [1] Her real name was Vercher. It is to be hoped that the other women in the novel—the mother of Rafael Brull and his wife—were not modeled from life.

The formula of heredity plus environment as the key to character is again used in *Among the Orange Trees*. The focus of the book is upon young Brull, lawyer son of the landowning political boss of the district. Rafael is dutiful, and although not interested greatly in the party, is willing to replace his dead father as *cacique* and continue to hold the electorate for the conservatives. We can believe in Rafael's early passion, an outburst nurtured by his stifling existence in a small town and his reading of Murger's depictions of bohemian life; but it is hard to forgive his lack of manliness. The author in one place mentions "the fluctuations of a weak and irresolute nature" (I, 638).

I *Passion in the Countryside*

The theme is revealed fairly early in the book, and is merely repeated at the end. "Crowned with the orange blossoms of the Huerta. Love had passed before him chanting the hymn of mad youth, lacking in scruples and ambitions, inviting him to follow her footsteps; and he had responded by throwing stones at her shoulders" (I, 674).

The woman who is the one great love of Brull's life—child of a neighbor who had left the town years before—has a heredity partly resembling his own. Her mother had been a healthy and beautiful girl of the Huerta, but her father, a rationalist doctor who had been a representative in the brief First Republic of the 1870's, irritated his smug clients by his advanced views, and his devotion to music caused him to take his daughter to Milan to be trained as an opera singer. They suffer poverty. She is raped by her voice teacher, and later becomes mistress of an aging baritone who promotes her career. Idol of the world's opera houses, companion of an ex-king and widow of a rich Russian count, Leonora has returned to her aunt's cottage on the banks of the River Júcar to forget the world and heal her wounds among the orange groves of her girlhood. Tall, opulent in body, with green eyes (an old Spanish sign of a passionate nature) and a casque of golden hair, she is the image of the Wagnerian Valkyrie that is her most famed role. But she hates men. She has never really known love. She lives only for the sensation of the moment. She repulses Rafael's boyish advances, but they become friends.

After Rafael returns from his first legislative session in Madrid, to which he had been duly sent by the electorate, he finds that the goddess has become, through the slow influence of the sun and air of the groves, awakened to a simple affection. She still treats Rafael as a child, and when, in early spring, he tries to force her love, she sends him back to his home, his mother, and his fiancée. But when the orange trees blossom, when the whole countryside is a white-and-green tapestry and the perfume maddens the mind, the lovers encounter each other in the moonlight and yield to a profound passion.

Their relations, however, cannot endure in the face of parochial spying and scandalized gossip. The old aunt is horrified at the youth's nightly visits. Don Andrés, old family adviser to Rafael's widowed mother and his political manager, warns that the young deputy must behave himself. Marriage to Leonora is out of the question. There is only one answer for them—the lovers must flee from the Huerta, to Venice, to Naples. They get as far as Valencia. The moment Rafael is separated from the arms of his Leonora, who now knows he is the one love of her life, he encounters Don Andrés, who has trailed the fugitives. Personification of overwhelming common sense, he argues with Rafael for an hour or two. The result is that Rafael sends a cowardly letter to Leonora and retreats toward a future of wealth, marriage, political success—and unhappiness.

The bereft Valkyrie returns to her old glittering cosmopolitan existence. She gets her revenge in the final chapter, eight years later, after listening to Brull make an important speech in the Congress. He is married. He has lost his youth, his good looks; he is bald, fat, self-deceived. Nostalgic, he becomes abject and offers to follow her around the world—if need be, as a servant. But the conflict of bourgeois versus bohemian is over. *Adiós, amor!* They have killed love.

In *Among the Orange Trees,* as in other Blasco novels, a man of infirm will is overwhelmed or destroyed by womankind. Opposed to his Wagnerian mistress are Rafael's mother, an ugly but wealthy woman of country stock, and his wife, a similar type whom he is expected to wed after his youthful fling is over—a wife whose "virtue is intolerable," who is "not a wife, but a female coldly resigned to the duties of procreation" (I, 672). One wonders again about Blasco's own wife—and his own mother, former Aragonese servant girl, of whom Martín Domínguez Barberá says: "She, so energetic and brisk, from whom surely Blasco drew the greater part of his genius, often showed that she was inflexible and abrupt with this son so little submissive to her wishes in matters of discipline, of rigor in duty, and of religious piety." [2]

Although Blasco seldom put his own career and politics into his fiction (for example, he never wrote a novel about his civic embroilment with Soriano), he maintains his irony by having the scene in the chamber of Congress reflect against the conservatism of his antihero. Rafael's big moment comes when he delivers an official response to the speech of a respected republican, an idealist of the Francisco Pi y Margall stamp who for thirty years has been demanding a happier future for Spain, into whose mouth Blasco puts many of his own party opinions. Why, for example, in the past generation have fifty churches been built in Madrid, and only one modern school? Rafael's lengthy answer, which draws applause and foretells his future as a staunch party hack, is a pompous outpouring of platitudes and a tired apologia for Catholicism as the heart of Spanish history and politics.

In *Among the Orange Trees* Blasco mingled naturalism with premodern symbolism, which he was to use even more successfully in books like *Cañas y barro (Reeds and Mud).* The orange tree stands for sensuality. Leonora herself, with her glowing skin and aura of blondness, is as tempting as one of the golden fruits of the Hesperides. As with eyes closed she is biting into an orange, with fragrant drops tingling her lips, Rafael loses control and attempts his first kiss—to be repulsed by having the amazon rudely throw him against the trunk of the tree (I, 616). In the spring, "Leonora seemed intoxicated by the virile perfume" of the orange trees, "those menaces of savage passion," but she refuses to be taken by force in their shade (I, 640–41). The aroma of full flowering, the scent of blossoms symbolic of a second virginity for this despoiled victim, sends Rafael from his bed to wander in the moonlight, and brings Leonora to a delirious yielding (I, 650). But as she says at the end of the book, "Above us now there is no moon nor oranges in flower" (I, 684).

The story of *Among the Orange Trees* was strong enough to have inspired a Greta Garbo film, *The Torrent*. The book's main charm today, aside from the depiction of such rural characters as Rafael's father the *cacique* or Cupido the town barber, is the evocation of the Huerta through descriptions. A few of these are the view from the hill of San Salvador; the flooding of the River Júcar and the midnight search for Leonora on its waters; the processions by which the superstitious townsfolk carry the bronze image of St. Bernard along the stream to cause the flood to abate; and the canoe trip to the idyllic island, after which the opera singer awakens the farm dwellers with her dawn hymn from *Die Meistersinger* ringing across the valley. The seasonal breathing of an expanse of orchards and the stifling stagnancy of a market town are forever preserved in this tale of passion in Valencia's countryside.

II *Proud Sónnica Rejects Surrender*

The fifth of the Valencian group, *Sónnica la cortesana (Sónnica the Courtesan)*, 1901, was Blasco's first plunge into the history of the region. It treats the most heroic episode in Valencia's past. As a truant university student, Blasco had often wandered upon the beach. To the north, above an expanse of orange trees, he could see a red range of hills, on the seaward side of which a thin, yellow brush stroke on the summit marked the ruined walls of a vast castle. It was Sagunto (the Roman Saguntum), the city that for nine months in 219 B.C. held out against all the troops of Hannibal and then committed mass suicide in one terrible night rather than submit to the demands of Carthage.

His imagination moved by evocations of ancient Spain and of the ships that had brought to the port of Sagunto the riches of those times, from Cádiz on the Atlantic to the far cities of Asia, Blasco interrupted his work on *Reeds and Mud* to write this novel about the tragedy of Sagunto. "Vast and monotonous studies" were required to enable him to recover the period background—the beginning of the Second Punic War—and he had to brush up his university notes on Latin and on classical lore. The result may not be an authentic recreation of the fall of Sagunto, but it is an entertaining piece of historical fiction that keeps one reading until the end, drawn both by the author's vivid descriptions of a little-known episode in Spanish history and by his depiction of customs and personages that might have been encountered in those far-off times. The modern deluge of lusty-and-busty novels of past ages may have sated our taste for a book which in its day was considered brutal and erotic, and it certainly is not favorably comparable with Blasco's works on the Valencia of his own era; but it may be noted that one recent Spanish critic terms the Sagunto novel, "symbol of loyalty to Rome," his "most illustrious and moral historical work, his first and most glorious blaze of genius." [3] And no one who climbs to the top of the broken citadel of Sagunto and views the partially restored stone coliseum can forget Sónnica and the other defenders of the city that was besieged by one of the most aggressive soldiers of all time.

Because Flaubert's novel *Salammbô* also deals with Hannibal, critics were quick to suggest that *Sónnica* was an imitation of an author Blasco greatly admired. And at times, his heroine and setting are strongly reminiscent of *Aphrodite,* by Pierre Louÿs. But as Blasco pointed out in a preface to a new edition in 1923, he had first promised himself to write a novel about Sagunto in his university days, and was not taking advantage of a *fin-de-siècle* literary mode that had made best sellers of Henryk Sienkiewicz's *Quo Vadis?* or of the works of Louÿs. His main inspiration, he revealed, was a little-known Latin poem by Silius Italicus, who was born at Itálica, near Seville, and who (according to Blasco, although classical scholars do not agree) wrote of the Second Punic War several centuries after the event. "Some of my secondary characters are taken from Italicus," Blasco said, "and certain scenes as well." The siege is also mentioned by Polybius and Livy.

The main character of the novel (unless he disputes the role with Hannibal himself) is a handsome and heroic Athenian adventurer, whose travels bring him to Sagunto on the day the city signs a treaty to obtain the protection of Rome. This city, with its busy harbor, its fertile fields dotted with the villas of wealthy citizens, its walled residential quarter and forum, and its upper defenses on an impregnable hilltop, is the most civilized center in the Peninsula of the time. Its population comes from a dozen stocks, but the principal rivalry lies between the native Iberians and the Greek merchants who have settled there and have tried to make the place a replica of remembered beauties from their distant homes. There is also a political split between those who trust in the power of Rome and those who fear the nearer threat of New Carthage, in which Hannibal, fiery son of the Barca family that had once subjugated many of the Iberian tribes, is rising to heights of warlike ambition.

Taking refuge in the temple of Aphrodite, the penniless Acteón encounters Sónnica, another Athenian who had been one of the most admired hetaerae of that city, but who had married a rich senator of Sagunto, had taken an Iberian name, and had inherited untold wealth at his death. Acteón is invited to her villa, and at once she passionately accepts him as her lover. That night a dinner is offered him which in all its phases represents an attempt in this province to enact the decadent orgies described by such authors as Apuleius and Petronius.

Exhausted, Acteón at dawn reencounters a mysterious visitor to Sagunto whom he recognizes to be Hannibal, spying out the land for his first attempt against the smug senators of hated Rome. Since Acteón's father had been a soldier of Carthage, Hannibal offers the young man, once a boyhood friend, a place in his forces, but Acteón decides to remain in Sagunto. The last words of the opening chapter—Hannibal's angry cry for vengeance against his family's enemies—are repeated at the end of the book: "Rome! Rome!"

Acteón enjoys the lavish life led by his beauteous mistress and her rich friends, and is a popular leader in the army being formed to defend the city. He visits the Acropolis whose foundation stones had been laid by Hercules after the death of his son Zacinto, from which the city's name had derived. He takes a tour of the back country with a friend who has become chief of a Celt-Iberian tribe, and the Athenian observes the crude life of those warlike early Spaniards.

The invasion comes all too soon. Hannibal's army—including Numidian cavalry, skilled stone-slingers from the Balearic Islands, catapults, elephants, and even a mounted troop of fierce amazons— overnight occupies and begins destroying the environs. They build engines that will, they believe, quickly overwhelm the citizens and slaves who have taken shelter behind the walls.

The scenes of the siege are the best in the book, and the reader gets a feeling of what it must have been like to live night and day for months under fire of a fanatically pitiless leader. Hundreds of Iberians flock to Hannibal's army each day. Direct assault on the city walls is overcome by the besieged, now united by danger. The breach made by the first attacking tower requires the defenders to retreat to a second line of walls. A higher tower is built that enables the Carthaginians to fire arrows and stones into the city while undermining the walls, but the new breach is defended once again, and the false rumor that Roman ships are arriving to attack Hannibal by sea inspires the people of Sagunto to a mad charge that nearly overruns the enemy camp.

The siege of Sagunto does not rival that of Troy, but several fine scenes remain in the memory. One is the duel between Hannibal and Terón, gigantic priest of Hercules, whose heavy mace cuts a wide swath of death. The queen of the amazons, who holds a despairing love for Hannibal, is one of Terón's victims. Unluckily tripping over a shield, the priest is stabbed by Hannibal, and the superstitious defenders take this loss as a symbol that the gods of Carthage will overcome their own patron Hercules. Sónnica, who has shared all her storehouses of food with the people, is the most inspiring and most unyielding among the defenders of Sagunto. But provisions are running low, and the two senators sent to ask for quick aid from Rome have not been heard from. Acteón is petitioned to go to Rome and ask the Romans to fulfill their treaty and help the dying city.

The chapter with a setting in Rome gives Blasco a chance to picture the city soon after its devastation by the Gauls. There Acteón meets Cato, tutor to the future Scipio Africanus and the orator who demands that Carthage must be destroyed. He also encounters the great Plautus, a Greek who had failed in his effort to set up a theater in Rome and, going into debt, had been sold into slavery in a bakeshop. Acteón's inspired speech to the Senate, pointing out the danger to Rome should she fail to defend her Iberian allies against Carthage, at first arouses sympathy; but Senator Fabius wins by counseling the sending of an embassy to chide Hannibal for his insolence.

Acteón knows at once that such slow tactics mean the death of his adopted city, but he returns to Sagunto and again fights at Sónnica's side. A terrible winter has passed in the besieged town, which miraculously still holds out. Two-thirds of the city has been abandoned to the hordes of Hannibal. Food and water are almost gone. Citizens and slaves steal about at night, seeking the corpses of animals to devour, and mothers debate which of their children is to be sacrificed to provide horrible provender.

For nine months the people have held up the march of the infuriated

Hannibal, future victor of Cannae, on the road to Rome. The last night comes. The survivors of the siege, spectral men, women, and children, aroused still by proud Sónnica, reject the surrender terms. To rob the victors of the spoils, most of them heap up all their jewels, garments, money, and other possessions in the huge bonfire on the Acropolis, and leap into the flames. Others, led by Sónnica, make a final sally, dying beneath the swords of the baffled barbarians. Mortally wounded, Acteón sees triumphant Hannibal, who dreams of overshadowing the memory of Alexander, galloping his horse into the sea and shaking his fist toward the east, where lies the sleeping enemy: "Rome! Rome!"

III   *It Also Is a Sin to Spit*

Of *Cañas y barro (Reeds and Mud),* Blasco himself said: "This is the work that retains for me the most happy memories, the one I composed with most solidity, the one that seems to me the most 'rounded.' " [4] Ezio Levi, an Italian critic, wrote that it "marks the climax of Blasco's art . . . perhaps the most vigorous work of modern Spanish literature, and in fact an historic monument, like *Madame Bovary* in French or *Anna Karenina* in Russian." [5] It is certainly the work that depends most strongly upon presenting a milieu broadly and deeply, and in it appear some of Blasco's most memorable characters. The story, not at all complicated in plot, well demonstrates the theme that misery often creates greed that leads to horrible violence. Although Levi felt that in this novel Blasco was rivaling Tolstoi, it seems more apparent that he was returning to what one Spaniard called the "sewer of Zolaism," and that all the characters are unfortunate victims of heredity and environment.

This environment, which Blasco does not depart from during the entire novel, is La Albufera, an extensive freshwater lake near the sea just south of Valencia. The name comes from the Arabic word for "lake," and long before Moorish days the region had been the haunt of primitive people who lived on the eels and tench abounding in the reedy waters, and upon the birds that sought sanctuary there by the milliards. As early as the writing of *The Mayflower,* Blasco had mentioned the Albufera fishwives who came to the Valencia market, "the wretched women, with weather-beaten and begrimed faces, their eyes burning with the strange glow of an eternal marsh fever, and their clothing smelling not of the healthy aroma of the sea, but of the effluvium of slimy ditches, the infected mud of the lake which, when stirred up, emits death" (I, 400). A week's stay at La Albufera on a shooting party gave Blasco the main materials for this final volume with a Valencian setting. It was finished at La Malvarrosa in 1902.

On an ordinary day, the visitor to La Albufera, lined with a maze of canals and patches of cane that is a species of bamboo, can look out upon its shallow waters, an unruffled sheet of steel, upon which glide the frail *barcas,* small shallops of the fishermen, and ask himself how anything of importance could ever happen here. But the lake's serene surface conceals many a snake-headed creature and horrid denizen; its mosquito-haunted mazes are treacherous even to the marsh dweller himself. And on a day of storm, when thousands of birds whirl bewildered, unsure which wind to trust, the fishermen hauling in their nets from the sides of their tiny, pitching craft look like an odd amphibian race, closer to the toad than to the man. Years of boring misery they may endure, but sooner or later violence will break the monotony and terrible crimes will ensue.

In the middle of the lake lies the island village of El Palmar, in one of whose *barracas,* shaped like overturned coffins with walls of reeds and mud, dwells the family of Tío Paloma, one of Blasco's great creations. He loves liberty and is proud of his honor. He is the oldest fisherman on the lake, and has devoted himself to gaining a living from its waters and from the birds that fly above it. He could remember the reign of King Joseph Bonaparte. As a young man he had guided Queen Isabel II in his *barca,* and had helped General Juan Prim to escape during a revolution. He knew every pool and shoal of La Albufera, and fought against the modern trend of filling in its edges with waste soil so that the fringing rice fields might take over the waters.

Unfortunately, he considers his son Toni, the only surviving child of the Paloma brood, a despised "laborer," who believes there is more money in rice than in eels and who spends his years toiling like an ant, hauling mud from the depths to fill in a broad area of shallow land to be reclaimed.[6] The old man has hopes that his grandson, Tonet, might follow the old ways, and teaches him the crafts of fishing and of poaching with his old blunderbuss. But after a few lessons Tonet reveals himself to be, like most people, averse to hard labor, and roams the lake and the Dehesa or common pasture ground with Sangonereta, son of the town drunkard, and a neighbor girl, Neleta.

Returning from Cuba after the war there is over, Tonet finds that Neleta's ambition has led her to marry Tío Cañamel, elderly and well-to-do proprietor of the main tavern in El Saler, whose income has derived mainly from usury and smuggling. In the yearly lottery by which the fishing rights to sections of the lake are allotted, Tonet wins the choicest spot. Tío Cañamel offers to finance the work, and Tonet, leaving the labor to his grandfather, makes much of the opportunity to spend most of his time in the tavern, on familiar terms with Neleta, who presides proudly over the bar. He seldom appears at the family *barraca* now, after his mother's death, in charge of an ugly, despised orphan girl, La Borda, who had been taken in as a slavey.

As time passes, Tío Cañamel, the rich man who cannot think of spending his money for anything but his appetites, dies of overeating and alcoholism. His will provides that, unless Neleta stays unmarried and has no relations with men, she will forfeit the inheritance to a hated relative. Her continued clandestine affair with Tonet, unluckily, bears fruit. Her swelling body, evidence that would betray her transgression, she stoically encases in a stiff corset, and in a prying village amazingly manages to bear her child secretly. As planned, she gives the infant to Tonet to be taken to Valencia and left on a doorstep. Exhausted and fearful, as Tonet in his *barca* crosses the lake populated with hunters and guides taking their places for the annual shooting spree of St. Martin, he weakens and tosses his bundle far into the lake.

A few days later, when he and his grandfather are acting as guides to a visiting Valencian duck hunter, Tonet's faithful dog, urged to retrieve a lost bird, brings back a ghastly burden—a newborn baby, toad-faced, swollen, partly eaten by lake creatures.

Tonet realizes that he has murdered his son, that life is empty, miserable, a trap. Overwhelmed, Tonet commits suicide in his *barca,* ironically using the gun he had been given by Tío Cañamel. To avoid scandal, his family buries the suicide in the filled ground that his father Toni had hoped to bequeath to him as a goodly inheritance. Before the grave is filled, La Borda, the servant girl, kisses the livid lips "with an ardent kiss, of immense passion, of hopeless love, daring, before the mystery of death, to reveal for the first time the secret of her life" (I, 927).

Again in this novel a strong and lustful woman overcomes a man who might have won honor in the world, could he have escaped from the milieu in which he had been reared. Neither Neleta nor Tonet are completely evil. But there is about them more than a trace of the effluvia of the ditches and marshes of La Albufera, home of a race which Blasco cleverly suggests resembles the flabby, slimy, serpentine eels and coarse-fleshed tench that serve as their chief food. Neleta is queen of the village, but she is unwilling to give up a tithe of her wealth, and thus plunges into a mother's worst crime.

In this novel Blasco makes us feel that we are acquainted with most of the people of the village of El Palmar, from the bird-hunting curate to the spiteful sister of Tío Cañamel's first wife. A memorable creation is Sangonera, drunkard son of a drunkard father, who resembles less the denizens of the depths than the birds that fill La Albufera's sky. Repeating a gospel he has invented to justify his refusal to toil he wanders like a sparrow, trusting that Providence will give him enough bread and wine to keep him alive from day to day. He is capable of seeing and touching Christ in the piny dunes of the Dehesa. But he is also capable, when hired as a substitute guide, of gorging himself on the rich foods in the *barca* and drinking himself into a state of nauseating surfeit that he finally cannot survive. Not even Sangonera is free from the greed that kills.

Apparent digressions in the novel often turn out to be anticipations. In the first chapter, for example, when we are taken on a trip from El Palmar to the mainland on the postman's sailboat, during which we traverse the region and encounter all the main characters, the story is early mentioned of Sancha the snake, witch companion of a shepherd of the Dehesa. At the end, this legend overcomes Tonet's mind, and he pictures Neleta as a giant serpent who symbolically is killing him with her ever-tightening coils.

Ever at his best when describing a locality he knew well, Blasco here gives us many vivid pictures of the Albufera: the *barcas* being poled across the reedy waters; the sails of a skiff, threading a canal, appearing above the reeds as if sailing on dry land; the solemnity of the annual lottery for fishing rights upon which a family's future may depend; the December fair of Niño Jesús; the iridescent wings of the marsh birds that are brought down during the fall hunting season.

Often the descriptions have a touch of warm humor. Over the basin of holy water in the church of El Palmar is a sign in Gothic letters:

> If by the lawful bonds of love
> Transgression is to be deplored,
> It also is a sin to spit
> In the mansion of the Lord.

Adds Blasco drily: "But if they admired the poetry, they did not heed the precept" (I, 856).

Spanish critics have been laudatory of the Albufera novel, although decrying the influence of northern naturalism. "Beneath the heat of the moving phrase," says González Blanco, "we see appear the powerful novelist, full of vigor, who has described, with dashing strokes, by dint of great energy, the joys and sorrows of a levantine village, those villages flooded with sunshine, their noisy wharves, their brusque and generous people ... and we laugh involuntarily on seeing this sordid silhouette of the evangelist, this preacher of the *dernier cri* [naturalism]; we laugh because we think that this determination of Blasco Ibáñez reminds us of a man who would like to wipe out the sunlight with a fistful of mud!" [7] Yet Eduardo Zamacois calls this "the best, in my judgment, of all his books." [8]

Foreign critics have been even more generous. An American, J. O. Swain, writes: "Blasco's Albufera, like Goya's 'Maja' or Velasquez' 'Don Baltasar,' belongs to the ages. . . . He has indeed preserved for the coming generations an idealized conception of a rather commonplace setting." [9] Gerald Brenan says that the result is "a novel in which the people really seem to be a spontaneous growth of the water and soil. Of all the 'pattern of culture' novels that seek to show how the life of a primitive community has been determined by its geographic environment, this seems to me by far the best. There is a unity of tone and color in the book that make it, with *La barraca,* one of the most aesthetically satisfying novels of the century." [10] The last of the Valencian novels is, all things considered, the greatest.

CHAPTER 5

The Novels of Social Protest or Revolt

BLASCO Ibáñez was to write, between 1903 and 1905, four novels in which the element of social protest or revolt is even more to the forefront than it had been in his earlier novels, and in which the settings shift from his Valencian homeland to various other regions of Spain. In some ways, too, these novels foreshadow the group known as the psychological novels, through the attention bestowed by the novelist on the development of character.

These four novels are *La catedral (The Cathedral)*, written at Playa de la Malvarrosa in Valencia in August and September, 1903; *El intruso (The Intruder)*, also written at La Malvarrosa, from April to June, 1904; *La bodega (The Wine Cellar)*, written in Madrid between December, 1904, and February, 1905; and *La horda (The Horde)*, written in Madrid between April and June, 1905.

In the two earlier novels the note of revolt is sounded against the Church. The exploitation of workers in the vineyards and in the large city is respectively condemned in the last two of this group. The setting of *The Cathedral* is Toledo; of *The Intruder*, Bilbao and the Basque provinces; of *The Wine Cellar*, Andalusia's Jerez de la Frontera; and of *The Horde*, the capital, Madrid.

Blasco wrote of this period in his career: "I simply want to make clear that I wrote all these books with sincerity and enthusiasm. We had just suffered a colonial catastrophe; Spain was in a shameful situation, and I attacked roughly, depicting some evidences of the comatose life of our country, believing that this might serve to arouse it" (I, 18).

I *What Must Be, Must Be*

The first of these novels was published in English in 1919 with an introduction by William Dean Howells, in the year before the death of this long-lived American critic. Howells lays stress on the poetic feeling, imagination, and psychological qualities of the novel, and praises its lack of "love interest."

The events of *The Cathedral* begin at the opening of our century with the return of Gabriel Luna to the cathedral of Toledo, where his family has worked and lived for centuries, and where he himself was born. He has returned to Toledo in order to die in relative peace, having left years before and having undergone many hardships abroad which have ruined his health. He finds a home again here with his brother, Esteban, who has not approved of the anarchistic, atheistic ideas of Gabriel.

The cathedral itself, traditional stronghold of the primates of Spain, is described in great detail; critics praise the novel for its circumstantial particulars, even though discursiveness is usually felt to detract from the interest of a novel. It is not surprising that guidebooks to Spain and, in especial, to Toledo, refer travelers to Blasco's *The Cathedral* for its historical and descriptive value. The setting is presented with such abundance of detail that it often adds depth to the impression made upon the reader by the characters in the novel. The reader becomes fully acquainted, for example, with the irreverent, mocking nature of Gabriel's nephew, the church dog-chaser, when he takes his uncle on a tour of the "lively things" (I, 979) contained in the grounds. The nephew, whose nickname is El Tato—that is to say, The Stammering One—brother—gives Gabriel a guided tour of the perhaps unedifying bits of artwork in the edifice, pointing out sculptures showing Adam and Eve unclad and Eve with clothes in disarray, as Adam forces himself upon her with such avidity as to appear to be biting, rather than kissing her breast (I, 980–81). Blasco takes advantage of the opportunity to comment significantly on this aspect of medieval folk art; Gabriel recognizes these sculptures as representing "the naturalistic simplicity of the Middle Ages, with all the directness with which the artists represented their profane conceptions, with the desire to perpetuate the triumph of the flesh in some ignored corner of the mystical buildings, in order to testify that human life was not dead" (I, 980).

Of almost equal interest, though not essential to the development of plot, is the information on the history of Spain's church music, which is part of the characterization of the chapelmaster, Don Luis, whose love for music is in accord with what we know of Blasco's taste. Chapter 4 expands on Beethoven's greatness, and the chapelmaster discourses at length in Chapter 5 on the contributions of Spanish composers. Shrewd insight into human nature is afforded by the reaction of Don Luis to the probability of the death of the cardinal. When the prelate falls ill, Luis is interested in his fate only because he thinks that this death would furnish a good opportunity for the performance of a famous mass with the help of a great orchestra recruited from Madrid, and Mozart's "Requiem" suggests itself as a happy choice (I, 1064).

Side by side with these informative digressions from the central plot are others of a more tendentious sort. Of this novel Blasco himself said that it had "too much doctrine." [1] Here didactic passages appear in which Gabriel preaches to his fellows his ideals regarding religion, government, and the workingman. Gabriel's ideology is presented by Blasco as a credible result of his life. Luna's precocious intelligence led him to the seminary as a student; political events in Spain at the time of his young manhood in the 1870's caused him to participate as an officer in the civil war, fighting on "God's side." Gradually he loses his seminarian's attitude, though not his seminarian's dislike of nineteenth-century science. Gabriel migrates to France and becomes greatly influenced by acquaintance with French Catholicism, much more progressive and friendly to science than that of Spain. He loses his faith in Catholicism as the only religion, and also his loyalty to the Spanish monarchy. He attends lectures by Ernest Renan at the College of France, and becomes familiar with the ideas of Proudhon, Reclus, Prince Kropotkin, and Bakunin. Finally, in the early 1880's, he goes to London, where he becomes intimate with a consumptive young Englishwoman named Lucy, who accompanies him to the Low Countries and Germany, lives with him for eight years, and then dies.

Gabriel returns to Spain, where—now barely forty, but physically an old man—he sees his brother Esteban again. Appalled by the poverty of the workers in the cathedral, he goes to Barcelona, where he participates in the workers' movement as a revolutionary anarchist. Two years of prison in Montjuich follow, and bring on tuberculosis. When Gabriel is liberated he returns to London, but the climate is too harsh. Poverty, imprisonment, and harassment by the police are his lot. He decides to return to Toledo to spend his last months there.

A summary of Gabriel's past life is narrated in Chapter 3 of the novel. It is consistent with the history of the closing decades of the nineteenth century, and affords as well a reasonable explanation of Luna's behavior and beliefs. He is the idealistic revolutionary, willing to undergo suffering for his convictions, but not, as it turns out, able to imbue his followers with all his ideals of social justice. The attempts of Gabriel Luna to convert his companions—the church's shoemaker, Mariano the bell ringer, and El Tato—form a main thread in the action. Gabriel speaks well; there is no doubt that Blasco enjoyed this opportunity of expressing his ideas through the lips of this likeable protagonist of *The Cathedral.*

Gabriel's ideas do germinate, but gradually the shoemaker, the bell ringer, and El Tato begin to push to extremes, in more practical terms than Gabriel had perhaps realized, the implications of some of his theories about equality and the distribution of wealth. Only too late—when they plan to steal the jewels from a statue of the Virgin in the cathedral—does Gabriel realize what effect his teaching has had on his pupils. Horrified by this unforeseen result, he tries to prevent them, and is dealt a mortal blow by the shoemaker, whose weapon is the chain of keys meant to keep from theft the cathedral's treasure. Gabriel's ideals—only partly understood—cause his death at the hands of the people whom he regarded as fellow sufferers, exploited by the Church, the Monarchy, and the Army.

Part of the sympathy Gabriel evokes, beyond the natural tendency of the reader to view sympathetically ideas and ideals held by an author, derives from the account of the relationship with Gabriel's older brother, Esteban, and particularly his warm human affection for his niece, Sagrario. She is the wayward daughter who has forfeited the affection of her father because of her decision to follow her lover—without benefit of marriage—to the capital, where, after a time, she is abandoned and forced by circumstances into the life of a prostitute. When Gabriel returns for the last time to Toledo, he inquires about his niece, and when he learns what has happened, he urges that she be found and—in a long scene, rich in argumentative and human power—persuades the embittered father to take the daughter back into the household. This is handled by Blasco with great feeling and skill. The father's forgiveness is not immediate nor complete, but his attitude gradually changes. The victory of Gabriel's ideals and of the natural love a father bears his daughter is shown briefly, subtly, clearly in Chapter 8, after the atheistic Gabriel has ironically exerted himself in order to earn some money by serving as bearer of the platform of the sacrament at the fiesta of Corpus. "But," runs the text, "as though he wished to acknowledge this exertion on his brother's part by something that would please him, when he returned to the Claverías he dropped his usual sullen face, and spoke to his daughter during the meal" (I, 1033).

The loving relationship between Sagrario and her uncle is another example of vague suggestion rather than insistent detail by the author. At the close of Chapter 9, Gabriel tells Sagrario that she occupies for him somewhat the same place Lucy, the Englishwoman, had held in his heart; this declaration of love on his part is enhanced by the background music—the chapelmaster, Don Luis, is playing on the organ

"Beethoven's last lament, the *Es muss sein (It must be),* that the great genius sang before his death, with a melancholy that made one shiver" (I, 1055).

II *Need for a New Religion*

The Cathedral is in the tradition of the nineteenth-century novel, both in Spain and elsewhere in Europe. The technique in the novel *La de Bringas* of Pérez Galdós, who virtually gives a separate existence to the royal palace in Madrid, is applied by Blasco in his depiction of the cathedral in Toledo. As a novel *The Cathedral* has invited comparison with Joris Karl Huysmans' earlier *La cathédrale,* as well as Manuel Ribeiro's *A catedral,* published in Portugal in the early 1920's.

The relationship of Vicente Blasco Ibáñez' *The Cathedral* to Emile Zola's *Germinal* has been obscured by the fact that *Germinal* deals with the social problems of miners and a strike, the topic of another of Blasco's novels, *El intruso (The Intruder).* Blasco provides his readers, however, with a clue to the debt *The Cathedral* owes to *Germinal.* In Chapter 1 Gabriel Luna reassures his brother, Esteban, that he need have no fear of Gabriel, since his mission is coming to an end: "You may rest easy, brother, I am a dead man; my mission is drawing to a close, but others will come after me and again others. The furrow is open and the seed is in its bowels. 'Germinal!' as a friend of my exile shouted as he saw the last rays of the setting sun from the scaffold of the gibbet" (I, 935).[2]

This passage clearly alludes to the conclusion of Zola's *Germinal.* Other echoes of this work may be found in *The Cathedral,* but the spirit animating this novel by no means reproduces Zola's intentions. Some of the similarities come from the fact that the social protest of both writers owes something to Pierre Joseph Proudhon and Mikhail Bakunin, and expresses itself in the prediction of revolution and a new world to come.

El intruso (The Intruder), 1904, continues the religious-social theme of *The Cathedral,* but the setting is now the province of Vizcaya, particularly Bilbao and its environs. Bilbao had undergone, in the last half of the nineteenth century, a great economic development in mining and metallurgy, so that an influx of workers from other parts of Spain, together with industrial development, had brought labor and social problems. Blasco suggests, too, that the development of Bilbao had also brought priests of the Jesuit Order, the group that represents the "intruder" of the title.

In Chapter 3 of this novel, Dr. Aresti, who is the spokesman for Blasco's ideas, mentions having read Maeterlinck's one-act play *L'Intruse,* in which the presence of Death, "the intruder," is invisible and yet is sensed by everyone in the houses she enters.[3] Blasco's treatment of his intruder, however, differs markedly from that of Maeterlinck. The gender of the intruder is masculine, to agree with that of the Jesuit priest, who destroys the long-standing affection between Dr. Aresti and his cousin, Sánchez Morueta.

There is, however, another intruder besides Death in the Blasco novel, suggested less openly and yet clearly enough by the novelist. This one is the so-called *maketo,* the poor migrant to the area, who has come from another region to work in the mines. The attitude of the Basque native of the region toward such workers is expressed in a conversation between Dr. Aresti and Goicoechea, an employee of Sánchez Morueta, in which is made clear the Basque devotion to the Catholic Church (and particularly the Jesuit priests) and dislike of the *maketo* (I, 1099). The word *intrusos* (intruders) is applied to these immigrants by Goicoechea, and he goes on to complain of the difficulty of finding good Basque names; everybody has names like Martínez or García, and more Basque is spoken in Madrid than in the Basque countryside (I, 1100). On the same page, Fermín Urquiola, the dissolute suitor of the daughter of Sánchez Morueta, reveals similar Basque sentiments, in expressing admiration for the Basque farmers and deploring the *maketos,* who have invaded the region and brought with them the worst there is in Spain.

The two types of intruder reflect two attitudes. For Aresti, and by implication the author, the intruder is the Jesuit priest, who has won the admiration and devotion of the Basques native to the region. But for these same people, the *maketo,* the migrant laborer, is the unwanted newcomer. Blasco implies that both the Jesuit and the *maketo* are intruders, but his sympathy is with the underdog, and not with the powerful, wealthy, insidious Jesuits. The social problem, that of the miners, again suggests that of Zola's *Germinal,* and the religious problem extends to that broached in Blasco's *The Cathedral,* so that *The Intruder* takes up again, in a sense, the questions raised in the previous novel.

There is more plot to *The Intruder* than is necessary for the presentation of the problems surrounding Toledo's cathedral in the earlier book. A brief summary may suggest that in this respect *The Intruder* has greater story appeal than *The Cathedral.*

Luis Aresti is a doctor, skillful and devoted in his attentions to the poor laborers of the Bilbao region, particularly the miners. His cousin, José Sánchez Morueta, is an enormously successful businessman, a tycoon of Bilbao shipping and industry. The cousins, brought up together, cherish a close friendship. During the course of the novel, the influence which the Jesuits bring to bear upon Sánchez Morueta's wife and daughter gradually overcomes his materialistic, independent, free-thinking spirit. The incipient love affair between Pepita, daughter of Sánchez Morueta, and a likeable young foundry engineer, Fernando Sanabre—neither a Basque nor a follower of the Jesuits—is destroyed by the influence of the Jesuit priest, Father Pauli, with the help of Pepita's mother. Pepita is thrown into the company of Urquiola, who lacks morals and has had a mistress even while he was courting Pepita; and her imminent marriage is accepted by her father by the time the closing chapter is reached.

Against this plot are projected the problems of exploitation of the workmen and the irritation between them and the Basque farmers, who are devoted to the service of the Virgin of Begoña. The Jesuits are hated by the proponents of social revolution and also by those loyal to Spain as a nation (in opposition to the independent attitude of the Basques). They are hated as well by opponents of the monarchy (in general, the Basques have been strong supporters of the monarchy and of the Carlist cause). The novel ends with the open confrontation of the Jesuits and their adversaries. Dr. Aresti gives medical aid to all the injured without discrimination; but his friendship with Sánchez Morueta comes to an end as the doctor spits in his cousin's face. The close of the novel gives the musings of Aresti on the future of humanity. Science and social justice will be the two sole deities of man's new religion.

Blasco found in the Basque province of Vizcaya the ideal setting for the social problems of the workers in the mines, foundries, and shipyards, and also for the continued attack on tradition, particularly in its religious aspect as exemplified by the Jesuits. Accounts of visits to the most important religious centers of that part of Spain enhance the reality of the setting. The reader becomes acquainted with the University of Deusto, partly through the expression of traditional, Jesuit-influenced ideas by a product of its training, Fermín Urquiola, and partly through descriptions of the monastery of Loyola; both are described with some of the same attention to detail that Blasco lavished on the cathedral of Toledo. At this monastery Aresti had met by chance his cousin, who was there to perform spiritual exercises.

The Intruder was not the first novel in which Blasco attacked the Jesuit order; he had in his youth composed a strong arraignment in *La*

araña negra (The Black Spider). Nor was this the sole Spanish novel
with an anticlerical aim; as early as 1876, Pérez Galdós in his famous
Doña Perfecta had implemented the influence of a bigoted priest and
his church on the mind of a susceptible woman, and two years later
Galdós in *La familia de León Roch* showed a home disrupted by the
vicious intervention of the clergy.

III   The Beautiful Little Duchesses of Madrid

The third novel in the protest group is *La bodega (The Wine Cellar)*,
1905. In it Blasco takes the reader to the city of Jerez de la Frontera in
Andalusia and its vintners, who extract fine wines from the grapes of
the region's vineyards. The physical setting has more similarity than
does Toledo or Bilbao to the Valencian homeland of the author, and
this novel, more than the two preceding ones, reminds a reader of the
earthy, rural atmosphere of the Valencian series of novels. Once again a
direct portrayal is given of the life of the peasant, as well as specimens
of Andalusian dialect.[4]

A rereading of *The Wine Cellar* by one who has visited the vineyards
of Andalusia brings back the color of the country better than could a
dozen guidebooks. This novel presents Pablo Dupont, owner of the best
vineyards and wineries in and about Jerez de la Frontera. He is shown
as a vigorous man, much under the influence of the Church—a tyrant,
but meriting the respect he wins from his employees. Blasco again
reveals the hard lot of the laborers, who are victims of a system in
which the land is possessed by a few despots like Pablo Dupont. The
workmen are underpaid, overworked, and even coerced into church
attendance. Virtually their only source of pleasure is drink. The novel
may be read as a tract against liquor and drunkenness, but this is a
somewhat superficial view.

As the plot develops, the laborers become aroused to indignation
against their exploitation. Fernando Salvatierra—whose name, meaning
"land saver," is symbolic—is the leader who expresses Blasco's ideas.
Salvatierra has his place in the novel as the idealistic revolutionary, who
never becomes a real participant in the life and attitudes of the workers
whose cause he espouses. He is somewhat like Gabriel Luna of *The
Cathedral,* cut off from the workers by force of circumstance.

One of the characters with whom we become best acquainted is
Fermín Montenegro, who works in the wine cellar of Pablo Dupont;
Montenegro is an admirer of Fernando Salvatierra and his ideas. Other
figures are Montenegro's sister, María de la Luz, who lives with their

father, the elder Fermín, at the Dupont vineyard of Marchamalo; and her young suitor, Rafael, foreman on the estate of Matanzuela, the property of Don Pablo's nephew, Luis Dupont. Luis is the embodiment of a type common in modern Spanish literature—the *señorito* or spoiled rich young man. María de la Luz is seduced by Luis when she is under the influence of wine. She becomes pregnant, and her brother tries to urge Don Pablo to exert pressure on his nephew to marry her. Don Pablo's solution is that María become a nun, but this plan does not match young Fermín's expectations. Finally, Fermín kills Luis Dupont when the betrayer refuses to marry María. Migration to the New World becomes the solution first for Fermín, and later for María and for Rafael, who has forgiven her through the good counsel of Salvatierra.

In contrast to the romantic plot are the harsh social conditions dramatized by a strike of workers over the whole region. Troops are sent by the government, and the workers band together on the Caulina plain. Part of the group enters Jerez de la Frontera and makes an unsuccessful attempt to kill their rich exploiters. The Civil Guard, better organized and equipped, breaks the revolt and hunts down the rebels. Blasco makes clear the tragedy of ineffectual leadership; one of his most poignant characterizations is that of the self-taught, idealistic farm boy known as El Maestrico ("the little teacher"), who is eventually sentenced to death for his participation in the uprising. Instead of killing the spoiled dandies of the jockey club or the theater, the strikers murder a harmless sixteen-year-old clerk. The scorn with which Juanón, one of the leaders, upbraids them cannot fail to excite a reader's sympathy: "Was this all they could do? Cowards! They had passed in front of the casinos, where the rich were, their real enemies, without its occurring to them to do anything besides shouting, fearful of breaking the glass windows which were their only defense. They were good only for murdering a boy, a worker like themselves, or a poor young clerk, whose pay was two pesetas and who perhaps was the sole support of his mother" (I, 1350).

The power of Blasco's writing is notable in the account of the events leading up to the death of the young gypsy girl Mari-Cruz. At the end of Chapter 5 Blasco describes a spree at Matanzuela, arranged by Luis Dupont. This *señorito* orders that a *novillo* or young bull be let loose from the stable. It chases Mari-Cruz, who faints of fright and becomes the victim of a long-continued fever. Her subsequent death and funeral comprise the main material of Chapter 6. Salvatierra diagnoses her illness as the result of tuberculosis. combined with alcoholism, but of course the fright triggered her collapse.

Again Blasco shows much sympathy for the underdog—in this book especially, the Spanish gypsy. These characters are human beings, not altogether admirable, it is true; but their suffering is depicted honestly and vigorously. Grief for Mari-Cruz leads an old gypsy woman to curse Rafael, who had not actually been at all responsible for her death. The woman truly predicts that he will learn that his sweetheart, María de la Luz, has been seduced by Don Luis Dupont (I, 1313). Afterwards, María will blame the wine, "the accursed wine" (I, 1337), but ironically the real culprit, Luis Dupont, is regarded as responsible neither by María nor by the old gypsy woman.

Blasco suggests indirectly that the downtrodden are so lacking in a spirit of defiance that they do not even think of placing the responsibility for their sufferings on their exploiters. Wine may have intensified their unhappiness, but the reader—if not the workers depicted in the novel—can see, with the help of Blasco's emphases, where the prime responsibility lies. It is noteworthy that Pablo and Luis Dupont are as blind to their responsibility as are the workers. The old order is accepted without question by people at both ends of the social scale.

The fourth of the novels of social protest, *La horda (The Horde)* 1905, takes the reader among the slum dwellers of Madrid, heart of Spain.[5] The protagonist is Isidro Maltrana, a favorite character of Blasco's who reappears in his next novel, *La maja desnuda (The Naked Maja)*, as well as in a short story, "El automóvil del general" ("The General's Automobile") and in the novel *Los Argonautas (The Argonauts)*. His first name, it should be noted, is that of St. Isidro, plebeian patron of the city of Madrid.

Maltrana is an intelligent son of a stonemason and a maidservant. His education has been sponsored by an elderly lady of some means, who dies before he completes his university education. Maltrana earns an income as a newspaper man and hack writer, and on one occasion ghostwrites a book on socialism for a senator, Don Gaspar, Marquis Jiménez. The journalist falls in love and lives with Feliciana, a factory worker and daughter of a poacher named Mosco. Maltrana's income is not sufficient to take care of both of them. Feliciana works, but becomes pregnant and falls ill. Her father is killed by the king's guards when he is caught poaching. Finally Feliciana is admitted to a hospital; she gives birth to their son and later dies. Her corpse serves for dissection in the medical school before burial in an obscure grave. The novel ends with Maltrana's decision to work hard for the sake of his son. He will fight for him, as he had not done for poor Feliciana, to whom he refers as the unhappy martyr abandoned by him.

Numerous subsidiary characters in *The Horde* are well drawn. Maltrana's humble origin and education permit him to encounter people of different strata of Madrid society. Through his eyes are seen the newspaper world, ragpickers, bricklayers, writers, a homosexual nobleman, poachers, a distributor of religious tracts, an antique dealer, juvenile delinquents in jail (among whom is Isidro's half brother), a shoemaker, gypsies, a doctor—in short, a true cross-section of the big city. One of the most memorable characters is the ninety-four-year-old dean of ragpickers, nicknamed "Zaratustra" by Maltrana. This name is bestowed because of the venerable man's wisdom; the allusion is to the sage of Friedrich Nietzsche's *Also Sprach Zarathustra.* The old man appears in Chapter I, which ends with a bit of common-sense philosophizing on his part, followed by the statement: "Thus spake Zarathustra" (I, 1377). When the ragpicker again appears, his repetition of the terse sentence arouses a humorous effect.

Critics have sometimes presented Blasco as a reckless propagandist, doggedly attacking the Church, the monarchy, and the army. This image is by no means accurate. Blasco gives, for example, a sympathetic account of the views of José, the bricklayer who is Maltrana's stepfather and who had formerly been a member of Spain's Civil Guard. José points out that priests can do no real harm to the workingman, and that the clergy and soldiery are needed for an orderly society (I, 1392–93). Maltrana is not convinced by such ideas expressed by his stepfather, but is impressed by the man's sincerity, and Blasco himself does not imply that he expects his readers to disagree with José, whose views are based on balanced experience, in spite of his savage enthusiasm for discipline and order.

No abrupt change was made in Blasco's development between the novels of social protest and the psychological novels that soon followed. *The Horde* was succeeded by *The Naked Maja,* which takes its title from one of the paintings alluded to in Chapter 10 of the earlier book: "Could Feli[ciana] see the meadows on the other side of the river? Well, there the rough characters and low-class Madrid women painted by Goya used to dance; there the great painter and the beautiful little duchesses who posed naked for portraits used to stroll" (I, 1490). In this brief reference one senses the appeal for Blasco of Goya's portrayal of Madrid's lower classes and his desire to offer another Madrid novel, this time concentrating on the artistic circles.

CHAPTER 6

The Psychological Novels

BLASCO Ibáñez quickly progressed beyond the use of fiction for social protest or revolt, and embarked on a succession of works usually labeled as his psychological novels.

All written in Madrid, they include *La maja desnuda (The Naked Maja)*, written between February and April, 1906; *La voluntad de vivir (The Will to Live)*, written between February and March, 1907; *Sangre y arena (Blood and Sand)*, written between January and March, 1908; and *Los muertos mandan (The Dead Command)*, written between May and December, 1908. The novelette *Luna Benamor*, to be discussed in Chapter 9, may also be considered as belonging to this group.

Some critics have thought that *Blood and Sand* should be classed rather with the novels of social protest. The present quintet, however, strongly stress character. Moreover, they reveal character in a specific setting. *The Naked Maja* is set chiefly in Madrid and completes the picture of that city begun in *The Horde. The Will to Live* reveals the natures of people in the upper social circle in Madrid and Paris. *Blood and Sand*, the story of a bullfighter, gives a picture of Seville in Andalusia, as well as of Madrid. *The Dead Command* has as its setting the Balearic Islands, particularly Mallorca and Ibiza. The action of *Luna Benamor* takes place at Gibraltar.

I *All Are in Love With Lucha*

All these works of fiction are alike, then, in having considerable psychological interest and take up, for more profound treatment than given them in earlier works, such situations as that of the adulterous husband (Juan Gallardo in *Blood and Sand* and Mariano Renovales in *The Naked Maja*), or of courtship (Jaime Febrer in *The Dead Command* and Luis Aguirre in *Luna Benamor*). Such topics are not absent from the preceding group of novels; Sánchez Morueta of *The Intruder* has a mistress; Luna Benamor loves Gabriel but does not marry him; Lucy and Sagrario in *The Cathedral* are lovers; Maltrana and Feliciana live together and have a son, without becoming man and wife, in *The Horde;* seduction, vengeance, and forgiveness are treated in *The Wine Cellar.* The effects of illness upon a person's character and on those dear to him are described in *The Naked Maja* as well as in *The Horde.* But the present group probes more deeply than the earlier one into human motivation.

The force of the title of *The Naked Maja* is made clear by Blasco in his introduction to an English translation.[1] The title is that of one of Francisco Goya's most famous paintings. The word *maja* is difficult to translate, but it denotes a Spanish lower-class belle. The type was depicted in art by Goya and in plays by the eighteenth-century Ramón de la Cruz.[2]

The plot of *The Naked Maja* is simple. A talented, successful painter, Mariano Renovales, marries Josefina de Torrealta, whose mother is the widow of a Spanish diplomat. Renovales finds a likeness between his wife's body and that of the naked *maja* of Goya's painting, and begs her to pose for him. She accedes to his request, but upon seeing the painting destroys it in outraged modesty. This act symbolizes her lack of understanding of her husband as artist.

The couple have a daughter whom they both love, but circumstances, particularly Josefina's attitude, lead Renovales to be unfaithful to her with her friend and schoolmate, née Conchita Salazar, Countess of Alberca. The daughter, Milita, marries a sportsman and automobilist, Rafael López de Sosa, rather than Soldevilla, Renovales' favorite pupil. Eventually Renovales grows to desire the death of his wife. Illness, long sustained and aggravated by jealousy, brings this to pass. Subsequently Renovales gradually becomes obsessed with visions of his deceased wife, who triumphs over him after death. He seeks to find a model whose body will be like Josefina's, but after he thinks he has found the right one, a cafe singer named Pepita who is known as the "beautiful Fregolina," he finds it impossible to continue painting when he sees her dressed in something his wife used to wear. Tragedy strikes when the artist, bewitched by the apparition of his dead Josefina, dies under a spell verging on insanity.

The natures of both Renovales and his wife are probed in this psychological novel. Josefina literally dies of jealousy. "It would be difficult to find in any novel," says one critic, "a better description of the progressive ravages of this emotion in a feminine soul." [3]

When Renovales is elected a member of the Academy of Arts, he is required to make an acceptance speech. He hires Isidro Maltrana to ghostwrite it. The appearance of Maltrana in this customary role links The Naked Maja with The Horde and the novels of social protest. Renovales' son-in-law is a graduate of the law school of the University of Deusto, but is depicted as more liberal than Urquiola in The Intruder. Allusions and digressions relating to art and music call to mind similar references and discussions in The Cathedral.

The Will to Live, dashed off in two months in 1907, has a revealing history. Its publication was announced and eagerly awaited by Blasco's fans. Twelve thousand copies were printed in Valencia. When Luis Morote, a well-known journalist, was reviewing the first copy, he was shocked to discover that Blasco had turned out a roman à clef, in which it was all too easy to recognize as its protagonist a noted professor, who presumably was associated with an equally celebrated group of South Americans spending a season in Madrid. Fearing that the supposed revelation of a clandestine love affair would arouse scandal, Morote persuaded Blasco to order that the entire edition be burned, at the expense of the author. At least one copy was rescued from the April holocaust, but the book was fated not to appear again until 1953, long after Blasco's fans could enjoy the narrative.

The key words in The Will to Live are life, death, and love. Blasco usually added a love story to his novels, but often this ingredient appears in episodic, subordinate form. Only in Among the Orange Trees and in Blood and Sand does the love element strongly rival that in The Will to Live as the main component of the action. Indeed, the broad theme of this novel is that love may overwhelm every other passion, including the desire to live, making death a happy liberation from an existence doomed by despairing love.

The main character is Dr. Enrique Valdivia, a biologist nearing fifty, a scholar first seen as a graying recluse who appears younger only when his eyes sparkle with what he calls "the will to live." As he says to his disciple at the end of Chapter 1: "Life at all costs, come what may; for the pleasure of living it, for the gusto of existence, for the satisfaction of having been born" (p. 36).[4]

But the self-sufficient doctor is swept up in the entourage of General Valenzuela, the dictator of a small South American country. The general, bored with ruling the land he had subdued by violence, is sojourning in Europe, depleting his country's treasury, dabbling in authorship, and trying to imitate his idol, Napoleon. He is accompanied by his chief executioner, Col. Amadeo Cortecero. Valenzuela's hostess is his "niece," an entrancing girl under twenty, with dark hair and golden eyes. Lucía, nicknamed Lucha, comes presumably of the family of the Spanish conqueror of the country, Santa María de los Andes, and is the daughter of a fallen soldier, a distant relative of Valenzuela. Both the general and the colonel are in love with Lucha, but she is wayward and enjoys flirting with younger men in their international circle. Dr. Valdivia also falls under Lucha's spell, and as the action develops this aging scholar becomes the victim of a devastating passion. The presentation of the main characters ends in Part I, when the doctor leaves to join the merry crowd that has moved on to Paris. "Thus departed the illustrious Valdivia from his disciple to encounter happiness and love, which strengthen the will to live" (p. 131).

II   *The Real, the Only Wild Beast*

The development of the action takes up Part II, with its setting amid the whirl of Paris. Back in Santa María, the general's absence has led to an uprising against him, and he has been reduced to the rank of head of the Paris legation. Heedless of politics, Lucha flings herself into a secret affair with the doctor, now living life to the utmost. They hold rendezvous in his flat, or take long walks. During one of these, when they pass the Morgue, the doctor reveals a method by which he could commit suicide so that no one would ever learn his identity. Their love is violent, but her attachment is mingled with fear, and his is corrupted by his jealousy of younger admirers. Just before the doctor is forced to return to Madrid, their emotions flare into conflict, followed by a reconciliation. Yet Lucha does not come to the station to see him off, and sadly he boards the train. "Was this to be the parting? Was this the way to begin, so coldly, the prime of his life?" (p. 253).

In Part III, the climax comes when Dr. Valdivia, after two months of gnawing jealousy, returns to Paris in murderous mood, to spy on Lucha. She is now dallying with a young poet, and when confronted by the doctor matches his quarrelsome attitude. During one meeting with the girl, he even strikes her. General Valenzuela's party has become supreme again in Santa María, and as he prepares to return to the presidential chair he proposes marriage to Lucha. Dr. Valdivia commits suicide, in the manner he had outlined, so that only Lucha is aware of his identity. The mere will to exist has been violently overcome by a passion that makes existence impossible. The repentant girl is the only one in the world who can go to the cathedral and pray for Valdivia's lost soul.

The dominant emotions of living, loving, and dying are shaded by others, such as fear, jealousy, and the urge to kill. The feelings of young and old are etched, and *joie de vivre* is contrasted with a pre-Freudian "death wish." The settings of the novel, as in the other psychological novels, are an integral part of the action, and the behavior of the vulgar followers of the cocky general is satirically noted. The characterizations are not so shallow as this brief account of the action would suggest. Several of the names are clearly symbolic: "Lucha," nickname of the popular girl, is the Spanish word for "strife"; Valenzuela might suggest "the little valiant one"; and Col. Amadeo Cortecero's name evokes his role as an enamored hatchet man. The power of Blasco's prose movingly comes through in this virtually unknown novel of his middle period, and presages his masterly *Blood and Sand.*

Blood and Sand, published in 1908, is the third of the psychological group of novels. It is one of the best known of Blasco's works, because it was several times translated and because it was a famous film vehicle for Rudolph Valentino. And it centers around the bullfight, for many years considered the Spanish national sport. It was written long before Ernest Hemingway made *aficionados* of everyone, and was the first popular novel to utilize this melodramatic scene since the days of Prosper Mérimée's *Carmen.*

Blasco's enemies accused him of manufacturing in this book an *españolada* or local-color Spanish piece with an eye to the export market.[5] But actually Blasco was not enamored of this brutal pastime; he would have agreed with his friend Pérez Galdós in terming the *corrida* "a continuous college and always open professorship of barbarity, insolence, and cruelty."[6] The novel is a detailed study of the art of tauromachy and the people associated with it; but it is not inside the arena that Blasco finds his true Spanish heroes. The psychological study of Juan Gallardo reveals a theme in which a brave young man, desperate to win quickly the success that is deemed greatest by the society in which he is born, is stricken down by the inevitable deadfall that life sets for such a victim of false standards.

One writer suggests that the plot of *Blood and Sand* might have been plagiarized from those of two other novels.[7] However, Blasco, as the author of *The Black Spider* and a dozen other tales of intrigue, had no need to borrow a story. Actually, the plot of *Blood and Sand* is as simple as that of a Greek tragedy. The story and setting complement each other quite naturally to reveal the theme almost inevitably through the characteristic actions of the protagonist.

The book opens with a day in the life of the most popular matador of his time—a day of *corrida* in Madrid. All is carefully presented—the nervousness, the dragging hours, the posing of Juan Gallardo as a popular hero, the ritualistic costuming for the battle to come, the daring exhibition of a killer trifling with death, the adulation of the mob. Then Gallardo orders two telegrams to be sent, reporting "Nothing new"—one to his wife Carmen, the other to a mysterious Doña Sol.

The second chapter offers a flashback to the birth of Juan Gallardo and relates his leap to celebrity.[8] Son of a poor Seville shoemaker, who dies while the boy is small, Juan escapes apprenticeship as a cobbler, roams the countryside performing at small bullfighting exhibitions, and by a courage born of desperation boldly escapes the drudgery and slow climb to full mastership in the arena. He is given public recognition by celebrated matadors and welcomed to their deadly galaxy of stardom. He marries Carmen, a Seville girl, supports his mother and his sister's family, and becomes the means of livelihood of his *cuadrilla*—picador, banderillero, and the rest. He gains wealth, buys property in the country, and wins friends, such as the Marquis de Moraima, famed bull breeder, and his imperious niece, Doña Sol. It is she who plays the role of *femme fatale* and thus satisfies her instinct by attracting and trapping him. Later, tired of him, she departs to seek other amusements.

The infatuation of Juan, who can do nothing but murder bulls with courage and skill, for this siren from a higher class becomes his ruin. There is public scandal and a home full of misery. The sudden departure of Doña Sol results in an agitation that causes Juan to suffer a bad accident in the arena. He spends the winter trying to recover, refusing to accept the suggestion that he curtail his expenses and face what seems to him to be degradation by retiring to the life of an ex-idol.

Doña Sol returns to Madrid, but this time she is cool. She does attend the *corrida*, however, on a day when all the worst things happen to humiliate the matador before the fickle crowd. His bravado leads him to show off wildly. The fifth bull refuses to be killed, because Juan, still recovering from his wound and agitated by the need for self-preservation, has lost the one quality a matador must have—the courage to close with the monster and strike home fearlessly.

The final chapter starts with bad omens, and Carmen comes to Madrid tearfully to wait in the chapel of the bullring for her husband. Again Doña Sol sits disdainfully in the box, and Gallardo, mad to wipe out the humiliation of the previous fiasco, takes chances that reconcile him with the crowd of *aficionados* who, safely in the stands, demand artistry and recklessness below. The final failure is not sensationalized or sentimentalized. Stricken by a goring that is scarcely visible to the onlookers, the great Gallardo receives his death wound. The mob clamors for another bull and another matador. Thus ends the career of the boy who lived a short life of mad aspiration, sudden success, vain display, animalistic infatuation, superstitious foolhardiness, and useless death.

The full-length portrait of Juan Gallardo—said to have been modeled on the popular bullfighter Antonio Fuentes, with whom Blasco traveled to many a *corrida* in search of the technical lore that makes *Blood and Sand* almost a textbook of tauromachy—is based on reality. Its verisimilitude was praised by a well-known matador of the time named "Bombita." The setting, mainly in Seville and Madrid, truly portrays the circle of *aficionados* and the sanguinary splendor of the bullring, the wiseacres of the sport, the hangers-on, the exploiters of the mania. Although Gallardo is the protagonist, the antagonist is not the siren, Doña Sol, but rather the crowd that makes champions and then destroys them. It is the fickle crowd that Gallardo must always entertain by his demonstrations of decorous courage, and his exhibitions must ever be wilder, leading him closer to dramatic death.

As Gallardo ponders just before his first accident: "He knew his public. One must cajole these citizens of the sun, a tumultuous and terrible demagogy that brought class war into the arena, but who could quite easily switch their hoots to applause as soon as a slight show of consideration flattered their pride" (II, 217). And at the end of the book, Juan's picador, El Nacional, laments: "Poor bull! Poor matador!" Then he hears the shouts of the crowd for new victims, new blood. "The wild beast was roaring—the real, the only wild beast" (II, 281).

III *Do the Dead Really Command?*

This faithful picador is perhaps the most admirable character in *Blood and Sand.* He has failed to win his sword because he lacks careless courage, but he can risk his body again and again to rescue his leader Gallardo. He is nicknamed El Nacional ("The Compatriot") because of his preaching of political changes that would improve the lot of ignorant working people like himself. He sticks by his ideals and tries to be a peacemaker. His altruism is contrasted with the greed of such leeches as Gallardo's brother-in-law. Other minor characters in the novel are of interest, such as Dr. Ruíz, whose specialty is curing gored bullfighters.

Sometimes Blasco is tempted to digress in order to portray local events. He has Gallardo join a religious brotherhood, and with this excuse proceeds to describe the entire pageantry of Holy Week in Seville and characters such as Captain Chivo ("Goat"), who comes each year to lead his bibulous company in the procession. Juan's religious role, however, might be justified by those critics who in recent years have found profundity in the mythic qualities of literature and who might see in him an embodiment of Adonis-Baldur, the youth who must die for the health of the tribe. The story of Theseus and the Minotaur, as is well known, may have been based on a Minoan ritual of leaping over wild bulls.

The greatest digression concerns the meeting of Gallardo and his friends with El Plumitas ("Little Feathers"), a dangerous bandit modeled on several outlaws that were reported in the newspapers of the time. Although El Plumitas risks capture boldly to attend Gallardo's day of fiasco in the Madrid ring, the brigand has no plot function in the novel and might be considered merely to add a curious figure to the cast. But here is another man of outrageous courage who, like Gallardo, has been driven by injustice to make a single-handed, doomed war against society.

Last of the psychological group, *The Dead Command* (1909), is one of Blasco's most stirring novels. It deals with the struggle of Jaime Febrer, the last member of a once wealthy noble family of Mallorca, to overcome tradition and to find love. The novel is divided into three parts, each ending with a statement which clarifies Jaime's attitude toward the power of tradition, as suggested in the title.

When the book opens, Jaime is living in the mansion of his forefathers in the city of Palma; he is in his mid-thirties, and because of lack of money has returned to his heavily mortgaged home, where he is cared for by a faithful servant, *Madó* Antonia.[9] As a solution to his financial problems, he thinks of marriage to Catalina Valls, whose father, Don Pablo, is a wealthy *chueta*.[10] The marriage between Catalina and Jaime is not approved by Antonia, nor by Jaime's friend and Don Pablo's brother, the retired sailor Pablo Valls. The Valls family is descended from Jews converted centuries ago to Christianity, but is looked down on by other islanders. Jaime decides to visit his wealthy aunt, known as the Papisa.[11] He expresses to her his desire to reform and to marry, and his need for help. She does not offer to help him and bids him farewell. As the first part of the novel ends, Jaime's thoughts are of the dead and their power. It is useless for the living to seek control of their destiny; even a modern, free man like Jaime must obey the commands of tradition and of the dead, whose attitudes persist and dominate the living.

In the second part of the novel Jaime Febrer leaves Palma for the island of Ibiza, to live on his property in a ruined tower built by pirates. Here he hopes to avoid the domination of tradition and the dead. He lives like a native of the region, and falls in love with Margalida, called "Almond Blossom," daughter of Pèp, owner of the estate called Can Mallorquí (Mallorcan Dog). Pèp is descended from peasants formerly feudatory to the Febrer family, and for him Jaime is still "boss." Among the suitors of Margalida are rivals: Pere el Ferrer, brawny smith, and El Cantó, a somewhat effeminate singer. By the end of this part of the book, Febrer has modified his conviction: the dead command only if people do as their ancestors did, but a man can control his environment and change his destiny. Upon arriving at this conclusion, Jaime goes to court Margalida openly, as she receives El Ferrer, El Cantó, and all the other suitors in accordance with local custom.

Pèp resists the idea that his boss should marry his daughter, an atlòta.[12] Ibizans, like Mallorcans, are too traditionally minded to accept the idea of such a marriage. During one Saturday of the open courtship, El Cantó sings a song addressed to atlòtas desirous of marrying gentlemen, and especially to a particular ambitious and heartless one. This slight on Margalida leads Febrer to a fight with the weakling, who threatens to kill him. Margalida's brother, El Capallanet, thinks that El Cantó's song was instigated by El Ferrer; if El Ferrer kills Jaime, El Cantó will be suspected.

Febrer is depressed by the complications of the situation and feels again that the power and authority of the dead are real; they do, indeed, command, and the living must obey them. Before Febrer is able to leave Ibiza, as he thinks he must, El Ferrer tries to kill him. In the exchange of shots, however, the smith is killed and Febrer wounded. Margalida, now in love with Febrer, nurses him back to health. At the close of the novel, Febrer realizes that the dead do not command. Life commands and, above life, love!

In his desire to heighten the interest of the novel, Blasco included the episode of George Sand and Chopin. The French woman novelist and the Polish musician spent the winter of 1838–39 together at Valldemosa, not far from Palma, capital of the island of Mallorca. One critic, analyzing the sources and function of this element in the novel, believed that Blasco had some reliable information about the Sand-Chopin stay at Valldemosa, but that—to no artistic advantage—he distorted facts.[13]

In his preface to The Dead Command (II, 283–84), Blasco indicates that he had gone to a republican meeting at the bullring of Palma in

1902 and taken the opportunity to tour the island. He became interested in the *chuetas,* or converted Jews, as well as in the site of the Sand-Chopin liaison, and decided to write a novel about these people. On his way back to the mainland he stopped also at Ibiza; the novel's projected scope was expanded to include this island as well. Six years went by, and in 1908 he returned to the islands to gather more impressions.

The shifting attitude of the hero with regard to the force of tradition is the psychological thread about which *The Dead Command* is constructed, but probably even more effective are the glimpses obtained by the reader of various aspects of the life of the people of Mallorca and of Ibiza. The social problem of intermarriage, the attitudes of the people toward the *chueta* and the *atlòta,* are characteristic of problems that need to be studied and resolved in many parts of the world today, not least in the United States. Blasco has an answer to the almost overwhelming force of tradition: the living must shape their own destinies, for they can control the environment in which they live. But the struggle of the living depends, in the last analysis, on love. Love and intermarriage seems to be the answer Blasco gives—at least to the romance between Margalida and Jaime, which leads to a happy conclusion and to the victory of living people over dead tradition.

CHAPTER 7

The Cosmopolitan and War Novels

BLASCO Ibáñez left for South America in 1909, and thereafter for six years was too occupied, as a lecturer and colonizer, to write novels. When he returned to fiction, his scope had broadened to cover an international range. "I endured in the desert," he recalled in 1918, "the life of the early *conquistadores* and of the cowboys as they appear in the films. And when, after passing five years of intense and energetic life—which, like the years of a military campaign, would count for ten or fifteen—I took up the pen once more, I wrote *Los Argonautas* [*The Argonauts*]." [1] This new group of Blasco novels is usually termed the cosmopolitan and war novels. It comprises, in addition to *The Argonauts* (1914), *Los cuatro jinetes del Apocalipsis (The Four Horsemen of the Apocalypse)*, 1916; *Mare Nostrum (Our Sea)*, 1917; *Los enemigos de la mujer (The Enemies of Women)*, 1919; *La tierra de todos (The Land of Everyone)*, 1922; and *La reina Calafia (Queen Calafia)*, 1923. Blasco envisioned a grand design, to write a series of novels about Spanish America, but the outbreak of World War I caused him to alter his plan. There is a natural transition from *The Argonauts* to the first of the war novels, however, and it is plausible to consider the cosmopolitan and war novels as forming a unified group.

The length of *The Argonauts* and its lack of a lively plot have prevented it from achieving the popularity that Blasco might have hoped for it. Apparently it was never published in English. In his 1923 introduction in the Spanish edition he says that this novel is the one he appreciates most; presumably his emotional response results from recalling a part of his life dear to him. Shipboard life appealed to Blasco's sense of adventure, and *The Argonauts* is a detailed account of a transatlantic journey that might also be read as a prologue to the disillusioned *Ship of Fools* by the American novelist Katherine Anne Porter.

I   *The Tango Dancer of Argentina*

The first chapter of *The Argonauts* presents Fernando de Ojeda, its protagonist, aboard a German ocean liner, fictitiously named the "Goethe," en route from Lisbon to Buenos Aires. The events in Ojeda's life before boarding the ship are given by the device of having him write a letter, full of reminiscence, to his beloved, a widow named Teri (an abbreviation of María Teresa), who does not have enough money even to support herself comfortably, and certainly not enough to support Fernando as well. He is forced to the decision to leave her for one or two years in order to make a financial success in Argentina, after which time he might return to Madrid and marry her. Isidro Maltrana, a character familiar to readers of *The Horde* and *The Naked Maja,* is also on board the "Goethe" and serves as a link between Blasco's immediately preceding novels and this group.

The remaining chapters of the novel are completely taken up with a detailed account of the trip, which includes considerable information of historical and geographical relevance to Spain's expansion to the Americas. Stops at Tenerife and Río de Janeiro; a detailed description of the ship itself, even of the ship's laundry personnel; the vaccination of passengers; festivities in connection with the birthday of the Kaiser (January 27); Neptune's court and the crossing of the equatorial line; a duel in Río de Janeiro; music, dances, love intrigues—all are related with lavish attention to detail and with both humor and dramatic effectiveness.

Blasco stresses the similarities between the passengers on board the ship, many of them immigrants seeking their fortune in the New World, and the Argonauts of Grecian mythology. The images of the gods adorning the ships of the first Argonauts are compared with the light of Hope, guiding the immigrants (II, 527). The early Spanish navigators are characterized as Argonauts who first violated the ocean's secrets (II, 643).

Fernando de Ojeda's name recalls that of his illustrious ancestor, Alonso de Ojeda (or Hojeda), a companion to Christopher Columbus, likewise an eminent navigator and *conquistador,* but less familiar to American readers than to Spaniards. Blasco likens Alonso de Ojeda to Achilles and to the Cid, Spain's great medieval warrior (II, 645).

Blasco's interest in informing his readers of his encyclopedic learning makes it natural for him to have Maltrana recall the first Argonauts, companions of Jason, as well as Apollonius of Rhodes, who put into verse the adventure of the golden fleece (II, 683). At the very end of the novel, the parallels are emphasized again. Maltrana again recalls the Argonauts: "We modern and common Argonauts [i.e., passengers aboard the "Goethe"] do not have to exert effort to go in quest of the golden fleece. It comes out to meet us. There it is. . . . See how it shines!" (II, 794—95). As he speaks these words, he points at the dome of the Argentine Congress building in Buenos Aires, golden in the rays of the sun.

The passengers are depicted with understanding and sympathy, even if they do not excite complete respect. Typical is Frau Mina Eichelberger, one of the women who awaken Ojeda's appetite for romance. His entrance into her stateroom, encompassed despite some reluctance on her part, is described with a mixture of cynicism and mock-heroism that successfully achieves a bittersweet effect:

Ojeda insisted: "Let me come in. . ."

He would attempt nothing against her will. He gave his word of honor. . . . And in the confusion of his excited desire, without knowing exactly what he was saying, without realizing how grotesque his oaths were, he sought new witnesses, new guarantors. . . . He promised to respect her by whatever she loved most in the world, by whatever he venerated with greatest admiration.

"I swear to you . . . by Wagner! I swear to you . . . by Victor Hugo!"

The door gradually gave way, as if these words had magic power. The pressure from outside, more and more energetic, helped it to move on its hinges, overcoming Mina's last traces of resistance.

And after it opened it shut suddenly, leaving the half-shadow of the corridor in complete solitude.

Poor Wagner!. . . . Poor Victor Hugo!. . . (II, 711—12)

The door becomes a participant in the seduction of Frau Eichelberger, and Richard Wagner and Victor Hugo unwitting witnesses to Ojeda's false promises. Frau Eichelberger's weakness is meant less as an indictment of woman than as illustrative of a common aspect of life on board an ocean liner.

It may be just as well that Blasco did not write a true sequel to *The Argonauts*. The vividness of the account of the days on board the steamer might not have been sustained were Blasco to attempt to follow the passengers through their later careers; some of the immediacy would probably have been diluted. The mood of the novel is one of hope and enthusiasm, but the all too human character of the passengers robs the novel of true grandeur. It seems as though Blasco has brought the golden fleece and the conception of the Argonauts down to earth. The size of the ship and the mass of immigrants make an impact, but the effect is created, as in life, by the accumulation of trivial details. And the novel illustrates the capacity of Blasco to derive his material from his recent experience; the reader feels that this account of shipboard life is the result of keen and energetic observation.

Another note addressed to the reader, appearing in 1923, shows how clearly Blasco realized that his inspiration for these novels came directly from his recent experience (II, 797–98). This retrospective note was intended to precede the next novel by Blasco, American in part, but primarily descriptive of the early months of the European War in 1914. He says that in July of that year, when he was a passenger on the German steamer "König Friedrich August," the last German passenger ship to land in France before the outbreak of the war, he noted forebodings of the conflict. The crossing itself, Blasco tells us, provided the source and inspiration for the first chapter of this novel, *Los cuatro jinetes del Apocalipsis (The Four Horsemen of the Apocalypse)*, published in 1916.

The chapter, indeed, echoes and supplements *The Argonauts*. Julio Desnoyers is the philanderer, making love this time to Frau Erckmann aboard the "König Friedrich August," a ship name which Blasco decided to retain. Julio's trip, like Ojeda's, was motivated by economic considerations, and an illicit love affair in each case was at the root of the financial problem. In *The Four Horsemen of the Apocalypse*, the ship carries the protagonist from Argentina to Europe, and in the second chapter Blasco gives a convincing portrait of Julio Madariaga, known as the Centaur, owner of a successful cattle ranch in Argentina.

The plot is constructed with great skill so as to combine in a reasonable way the New World, France, Germany, the events of the war, and a sense of history over all. A flashback sums up the chief events in the life of Julio Desnoyer's father, a Frenchman named Marcelo Desnoyers, who was a young man eligible for military service in 1870, when France and Germany were at war. His disapproval of the war and the French Empire caused him to leave France for Argentina. Some ten years later, he began to work for Julio Madariaga, a Spaniard who had migrated to Argentina. He made his fortune and life there, marrying a *mestiza* who had become the mother of his two daughters. After five years of working for Madariaga, Marcelo falls in love with, and marries, Luisa, his employer's older daughter. Another employee, a German immigrant named Karl von Hartrott, son of a German general in the

War of 1870, falls in love with Madariaga's other daughter, Elena, to
the displeasure of her father.

Eventually children are born to the daughters: Julio and Chichí
Desnoyers, Julius (later a university professor), Otto (later a military
captain) von Hartrott, and several others. After Julio Madariaga's death,
the Desnoyers family returns to France after having settled for a time in
Buenos Aires; the Hartrott side of the family goes to Berlin.

Julio Desnoyers is pleasure-loving and an expert dancer of the tango.
His philandering desires lead to a five-month trip to Argentina shortly
before the outbreak of the war.

II *The "Blue Beast" and Mata Hari*

The effect of the war on the various people who take part in the
novel is varied. Marcelo Desnoyers is led to regret that he deserted
France in 1870, and wishes that he might play an active part in the
defense of his country. Mme Margarita Laurier, whose husband, an
engineer who entered the service of France in the war and had been
wounded, gives up the idea of marriage with Julio and returns to her
husband, to whom she becomes devoted, as if to atone for her
faithlessness. Frau Elena von Hartrott loses two of her sons in the war,
and a third son is wounded. Chichí Desnoyers marries René Lacour,
seriously wounded in battle, and determines to dedicate herself to his
care. The war eventually causes Julio Desnoyers to enter the service of
France, even though as an Argentinian he is not obliged to do so. The
war is effective in transforming people; Julio's sacrifice of his life in the
struggle against the Germans on the battlefield, as developed by Blasco,
seems psychologically natural.

The immediacy of the novel, its remarkably detailed and lifelike
account of the Battle of the Marne, its somewhat heavy-handed but
sincere depiction of the least sympathetic aspects of German *Kultur*
and militarism, the admiration displayed by Blasco for the heroism of
the French under attack and the self-sacrificing spirit particularly of
French women, who rise to the cruel demands of war—all these may
account for the tremendous success of this novel, not only in Spanish,
but also in English translation. In 1921, one of Hollywood's most
successful motion pictures of all time was the version directed by Rex
Ingram in which Rudolph Valentino, Alice Terry, and Wallace Beery
were starred. Some four decades later, in 1962, a new version was made
of *The Four Horsemen of the Apocalypse* which starred Glenn Ford,
Ingrid Thulin, and Charles Boyer. The psychological skill of Blasco was

so great that it was possible for the era in which the events of the war took place to be changed; the second film transferred the events to World War II, and the anti-Prussian propaganda still seemed appropriate, as did the theme of the courageous attitude of the French under attack by the Germans.

The title of the novel and film is another example of Blasco's desire to draw symbolic parallels between the past and the period he depicts. The four horsemen of the Apocalypse are the scourges of the earth mentioned in the scriptural Book of Revelation: Plague, War, Hunger, and Death, as explained by one of Blasco's interesting didactic, philosophizing characters, Tchernoff (II, 871). Blasco refers to the "four horsemen" several times in the novel, not only in the Bible, but also in the engravings of Albrecht Dürer in a book printed in 1511, with Latin text and the title *Apocalipsis cum figuris*. It is Tchernoff who gives us much of the intellectual attitude that Blasco must have held as he wrote the novel. Through this Russian we learn that the revolutionary father of anarchism wept with emotion at hearing Beethoven's *Ninth Symphony*, conducted by his young friend, Richard Wagner; Tchernoff quotes the statement made by M. A. Bakunin, as he clasped the German conductor's hand: "When our revolution comes and what exists perishes, this must be saved at all costs" (II, 867). Blasco's dislike for *Kultur* did not extend to a lack of admiration for Beethoven and Wagner.

The president of France, Raymond Poincaré, invited Blasco to visit the scene of the Battle of the Marne in the hope that the Spanish writer would be able to make use of his experience to create something that might help the cause of France. And certainly *The Four Horsemen of the Apocalypse* must be counted as an impressive feat of propaganda. The sincerity, energy, passion, and psychological truth of the novel enhance its value, and even in a period when two world wars have receded into the past a reader can find aspects of it that are timely.[2] It is hopeful to think that some of the pacifists and dissenters of the present may find, years later, like Marcelo Desnoyers, that their attitude toward their home country has changed. In any case, Blasco resists the temptation to pass judgment on Marcelo's position; our idea of whether he is more or less admirable in 1914 than in 1870 comes from our assessment of his character and feelings as he himself expresses them. It is hard to know, in fact, whether Blasco expects a reader at the end of the novel to share the pessimistic views of Don Marcelo Desnoyers, who is certain that the four horsemen will walk the earth again, no matter what the outcome of the war is, or the more zest-filled attitude of his daughter Chichí, for whom the graves of the dead are a stimulus to thoughts of the living.

In the following year, between August and December, 1917, Blasco wrote his second war novel: *Mare Nostrum (Our Sea)*. The title is not Spanish, but Latin, and has a double application. First, it indicates the setting of the novel, the Mediterranean Sea, which was affectionately called *mare nostrum*, "our sea," by the Romans. Blasco introduces the sea with attributes of a semidivine being: "... a type of blue beast, powerful and of great intelligence, a sacred animal like the dragons and serpents worshipped by certain religions, who see in them sources of life" (II, 1013).

Second, it is the name given by the hero of the novel, the sea captain Ulises Ferragut, to the ship bought by him, which had previously been named the "Fingal." It is this ship which he uses in order to help supply German submarines with oil in the Mediterranean during the middle years of the war. Characters in the novel in several cases are given symbolic names which are reminiscent of the way in which Blasco saw in the European immigrants to Argentina the Argonauts of ancient Greece. Ferragut's uncle, a doctor and man of the sea, is called "The Triton" (II, 1006). The Triton is undoubtedly another of Blasco's most interesting creations; his love for the Mediterranean Sea is physical and unforgettable. Esteban, the captain's son, is a new Telemachus, whose father, Ulises, like Ulysses of old, has been away from home and family far too long (II, 1124).

The woman who, as Circe did to Ulysses, keeps Ulises from returning home more quickly is known in the novel as Freya Talberg, though she tells us that her real name is Beatriz (II, 1169). Freya Talberg is also equated with the goddess Freya (II, 1062). She is a spy for the German cause, who persuades Captain Ferragut to use the "Mare Nostrum" to help supply German submarines. She is an interesting figure, and Gascó Contell states that Blasco created her before he knew anything about the famed spy known as Mata Hari, but that before the novel was completed, he was able to incorporate historical details about the trial and execution of the real spy into his novel.[3]

III *America the Friendly, the Generous*

Whereas in *The Four Horsemen of the Apocalypse* Blasco depicted wartime France on land, in *Mare Nostrum* the sea and shipping, as well as activity in ports, provide the setting. The propaganda in this work is particularly directed against the horrors of submarine warfare. Esteban

Ferragut is blown up on board the "Californian," torpedoed by a German submarine. His father sees survivors from the "Californian" rescued by the French steamer he has boarded in order to go to Marseilles from Naples. This event leads him to determine to seek vengeance against the submarines. At the same time he blames himself, through his weakness in giving in to the wiles of Freya Talberg, for the death of his son.

Some criticism has been directed against the encyclopedic detail included in *Mare Nostrum* by the author. The description of the aquarium of Naples, in Chapter 5, is perhaps the best example. As a description of the aquarium and its tenants it is masterly, and it also provides a picturesque setting for the romantic byplay between Freya and Ulises. The effect on Freya, too, at the sight of the crab being fed to the octopus, reveals the animallike vitality and intensity of this woman, and makes it easy to understand how Ulises could become a victim of her charm and sensuousness. There is vitality as well as melodrama in the comparison of the octopus to Freya, and of the doomed crab to Ulises, and the effect of Freya's kiss is inevitable. Chapter 5 closes as follows: "And he let himself be carried away by the caress of the wild animal, with his thought lost and his body inert and resigned, just like the shipwrecked man who descends and descends the infinite layers of the abyss without ever reaching the bottom" (II, 1077).

The lengthy description of the aquarium in Naples does serve an artistic function, but it is possible that some shortening of this chapter would have kept narrative and setting in better balance. In answer to this criticism, however, it must be admitted that Blasco makes clear the relevance of the octopus and the crab not only to an understanding of the characters of Freya and of Ulises, but also to the seduction of the latter by the exciting "wild animal." [4]

At least two film versions of *Mare Nostrum* brought the novel to screen audiences. In 1926 an American production starred Alice Terry, and in 1948 María Félix, Fernando Rey, and Nerio Bernardi were the leading actors in the Mexican production.

The last of Blasco's three novels dealing with the World War of 1914–1918 is *Los enemigos de la mujer (The Enemies of Women)*, written between January and July, 1919. In 1923 it was made into a Hollywood motion picture, with Lionel Barrymore, Alma Rubens, and William Collier, Jr. in the cast. *The Four Horsemen,* the first of the trilogy, dealt with the land war in France; the second, *Mare Nostrum,* with the submarine warfare in the Mediterranean; *The Enemies of*

Women deals especially with the effect of the war on people who had sought to escape the hardships of war by retreat to neutral ground, and who obtained their satisfaction in life from gambling. Blasco became ill as a result of overwork in the abnormal conditions of wartime Paris during the four years of the war, and went to Monaco and Monte Carlo in order to restore his health. His active mind again observed people whose situation appealed to his novelistic instincts, and the result was this book, in which the conclusion of hostilities and the arrival of American soldiers on the scene serve to relate the novel to the war.

The book opens with the statement made by the Russian prince, Miguel Lubimoff, whose income has been severely reduced and who is forced by circumstances to live in his Villa Sirena in Monte Carlo: "A man's great wisdom is that he does not need a woman" (II, 1218).

The attitude this statement reflects leads him to gather together a group of men who live as his guests in the villa. Besides the "ruined" prince, the group consists of Atilio Castro, a Spanish dilettante distantly related to the prince; Teófilo Spadoni, a pianist of humble Italian parentage who always plays the number five at the casino; Dr. Carlos Novoa, a scientist engaged in research at the Oceanographic Museum in Monaco; and the prince's companion and "chamberlain," known as "Colonel" Marcos Toledo. The bargain they make to band together in a life to be spent completely without women, under the name of "the enemies of women," suggested by Atilio Castro, proves impossible to keep, and in the course of the novel the group breaks up. Thus, *The Enemies of Women* is by no means devoid of romantic intrigue and of interesting women characters.

Alicia, Duchess of Delille, is one of Blasco's most vivid feminine characters. She is athletic and promiscuous, but capable of great love; Blasco emphasizes a similarity between her and Helen of Troy. It is Alicia herself who states that the most beautiful and aptest thing ever written is the passage in Homer about "the old men's bench," where the Trojans, rapt in wonder, watched Helen as she passed by (II, 1251; also 1289, 1381, 1432). Alicia has separated from her husband because of her promiscuous interest in other men, but she has one son, Jorge, whose surname, taken from that of a married couple in the employ of the duchess, is Bachellery. For some time, Alicia had lived with her son; the world at large thinks that they are lovers, rather than mother and son. During the war, Jorge Bachellery became a pilot, and later a prisoner of the Germans. Because of her love for her son, Alicia enlists the help of the prince, whom she has known since her childhood days. Between them a love-hate relationship has developed. She needs to find out in what prison camp her son is held, and also needs money and influence to have her son returned to her. The efforts of Prince Miguel are fruitless, and Alicia receives word of the death of Jorge.

The prince courts Alicia, but she is not willing to yield to him, although she is grateful for his desire to be of help. Years before she had attempted to seduce him, and he had not responded to her advances, much to her astonishment and anger. "You are the only person who could do what you have done," she says, cuttingly, upon dismissing him. "Now I see clearly. I hate you just as you hate me. My caprice was stupid. You have permitted yourself a luxury that nobody in the world will be able to imitate. If I were younger, I would give you another whipping like the one in the Bois; but lacking it, rest assured that I am repeating to you what I said then" (II, 1252).

After receiving the news of her son's death, Alicia tries to turn her attention to a wounded officer, toward whom she has a maternal affection. Unfortunately, Prince Miguel misunderstands and, moved by jealousy, asks the lieutenant, Antonio Martínez, to stop visiting the duchess. This action leads to a duel, in which, however, neither the prince nor the lieutenant is killed, but which causes Martínez to think of the duchess rather as a woman to make love to than as a foster mother. Alicia tries to commit suicide, and eventually dies, infected with tetanus from a surgical knife when serving in a military hospital.

American readers will appreciate the attitude toward American involvement in the war expressed in the novel. Blasco's admiration for the United States and for President Wilson is undeniably and forcefully portrayed. Let the following passage serve as illustration: "A people has just risen above the peoples of the earth. Never has a similar rise been known in history. It assumes the lead through friendliness, through its generous acts, through the beneficent strength of its activity; not through fear, the basis of every greatness in the past" (II, 1438).

IV *California, the Legendary Island*

After completion of the war trilogy, Blasco was able to turn back to his South American series, although somewhat deflected from the original scheme. From February to April, 1922, he completed *La tierra de todos (The Land of Everyone)*. The setting of this novel evolved from Blasco's experience in undertaking the foundation of two colonies in Argentina, one of them in the Río Negro region of Patagonia. It is this part of Argentina, with its promise as well as difficulties for new immigrants, that is "the land of everyone," so termed by Manuel

Robledo, an engineer and former fellow student of the Marquis de Torrebianca, when persuading the latter to try to make a new life for himself in the New World.

This novel was made into a motion picture in 1926 under the title of *The Temptress,* featuring Greta Garbo and Antonio Moreno. "The temptress" is an apt description of the chief feminine character in the novel, who was the promiscuous, selfish wife of the marquis, and who is largely responsible for their economic ruin in Paris as the novel's action begins. Her beauty had won her the epithet of *la Bella Elena,* "the fair Helen," thus relating her, by the implied comparison with Helen of Troy, to Alicia, the Duchess of Delille of *The Enemies of Women.*

The marchioness is completely selfish, and delights in making use of her beauty and wiles to captivate men and lead them to their downfall. The new community is gradually ripped apart by the lack of harmony Elena's machinations create; the irrigation and reclamation projects are postponed, and unhappiness, suspicion, fights, and death ensue.

Typical of Elena's ruthlessness is her behavior toward the "Flor de Río Negro" (Flower of Black River), Celinda Rojas, a rancher's eighteen-year-old daughter in love with Robledo's partner, a *gringo*—as foreigners are called in Argentina—named Ricardo Watson, a graduate of the University of California at Berkeley. Elena plots to have Celinda kidnapped and killed; Celinda, however, is rescued from her kidnapper.

Blasco suggests that Elena is the prey of forces beyond her control: "Often in her life she had felt the same surprise at her own acts, as if there were inside her two opposing personalities, one of which inspired the other with horror" (III, 126).

Elena is equated by Blasco with the evil demon of local superstition, the *Gualicho*: "*Gualicho,* the terrible demon of the pampas expelled at the same time as the natives, had returned to these lands that belonged to him, conquering them again" (III, 77).[5]

Robledo gives his view of Elena's character: "I do not think that she is completely evil. She is an impulsive woman, with untrained passions, who sows evil often without being aware of it, for she puts all her attention on herself, thinking that she is the center of existence. If she were rich, perhaps she would be good; but she is not acquainted with modesty and is incapable of accepting sacrifice. She wants so many things and has so few!" (III, 105).

In any case, Elena's deficiencies in character result in her nearly complete ruin; at the end of the novel Robledo recognizes her along the Boulevard Rochechouart, a streetwalker, craving whiskey although not drugs. After they converse and reminisce, Robledo comments: "And this is Elena who, like the Helen of the old poet, began the war between men in a corner of the earth" (III, 150).

The description in this novel of the new settlement in Patagonia and the people of many nationalities who live there is well sustained. Blasco takes pains to remind us that the settlement is "everybody's land." Robledo repeats this sentiment in one of his storytelling sessions at the house where the marquis, Robledo, and Watson make their home upon their arrival at Fuerte Sarmiento (III, 51). The historical and geographical setting of the settlement is also presented to the reader bit by bit, and with considerable naturalness, by different characters and without the lengthy digressions that for some critics have been defects in such novels as *The Cathedral, The Argonauts,* or *Mare Nostrum.*

Californians, in particular, are interested in Blasco's *La reina Calafia (Queen Calafia),* 1923, the third of his American novels. Actually this novel combines American with European settings, and also foreshadows the more purely historical novels that followed.

The title serves a variety of purposes. In Chapter 3, Blasco refers to the early sixteenth-century Spanish chivalric novel by Garci Ordóñez de Montalvo—a sequel to the more famous *Amadís de Gaula*—the title of which is *Las sergas de Esplandián.*

Calafia, according to the Esplandián novel, was the name of the queen who ruled over a group of Amazons on a legendary island named California and who led her female subjects to take part in a siege of Constantinople. There she carried on a hopeless pursuit of Esplandián, son of Amadís of Gaul. Thus the title suggests a noble Amazon, unsuccessful in love. Likewise, the name of the legendary island causes modern readers to think of that part of the New World, first explored by Spaniards.[6] Chapter 3 of the novel is taken up by a professor who virtually gives a history of California, which picked up that name in the time of Hernán Cortés, conqueror of Mexico. The power of the name taken from a popular romance encouraged the later idea that California was an island.

V *No Longer an Amazon Queen*

Blasco weaves much California history into his story even into the twentieth century. He gives much space to the faithful Concha Argüello, who waited thirty-six years for the return of her Russian lover Rezanov, who had been killed in Siberia a few months after leaving her (III, 186 ff.). He points out that the Bay of San Francisco, ironically, was discovered by a land expedition (III, 178). He laments that few

Americans know the achievements of Don Bernardo de Gálvez who, as the young governor of Louisiana, in 1780 drove the British from Mobile and Pensacola (III, 179—81). And he comments that the name given by Californians to the city of San Francisco is "Frisco"! (III, 185).

This historical account of California's past serves to introduce Concha Caballos, daughter of one of the descendants of the early Spanish settlers. She is, as it were, a reincarnation of Queen Calafia—similar in a number of ways, in beauty, strength, and other admirable qualities. It is the university professor, Antonio Mascaró, who calls her Queen Calafia when she first appears (III, 159; see also 193, 194, 196, 197). Actually, however, she is the widow of a distinguished American diplomat named Douglas, twenty-five years her senior. Very wealthy and still beautiful, she goes to Madrid, where she again meets Ricardo Balboa, an engineer with whom she had fallen in love in her youth, when he was a young engineer in Mexico. In the intervening years, Ricardo and his Mexican wife had a son named Florestán, who like his father was an engineer and who had developed a romantic attachment for Consuelito Mascaró, daughter of Balboa's friend Professor Mascaró. Florestán falls in love with Consuelito, and she with him. As in the old romance, the affair between Mrs. Douglas (the modern Calafia) and Florestán (the modern Esplandián) does not end in their marriage.

After Florestán and Mrs. Douglas are attracted to each other, a duel takes place between Florestán and another of her suitors, the Marquis de Casa Botero. Florestán is seriously but not fatally wounded. Not caring about what people might say, Mrs. Douglas devotedly nurses Florestán, repeating from time to time two sentences that make clear her feelings: "Poor boy! . . . What infamy!" (III, 225—26).

The tone is noble and almost maternal. When the Marquis de Casa Botero confronts Mrs. Douglas, the reader is prepared for her reaction, which is in accord with her Amazon-like qualities. Casa Botero explains to Mrs. Douglas that any man who makes bold to be his rival for her affections must suffer death. The youth of Florestán makes it possible for Casa Botero not to kill him, but merely to teach him a good lesson with a chest wound. Mrs. Douglas interrupts his explanations with a blow to the face, characterized as masculine and athletic. Casa Botero, in surprise, raises his hand in self-defense, to the delight of Mrs. Douglas, who is pleased to see that Casa Botero regards her as an equal. She deals him a mighty blow on his face with her right hand, and her ring cuts his lips. A third blow seems to crack his jaw, and he falls to the floor. When he fails to rise, she proudly places her foot on his head so that the high, sharp heel of her shoe is on top of the Marquis' mouth (III, 228).

Consuelito Mascaró, who still loves Florestán, begs Mrs. Douglas to give him up. Consuelito admires Mrs. Douglas, but feels that she should marry one of the older men, who should appeal to the millionairess. Consuelito feels that there is room in her life for only one man, Florestán, and that she herself could never compete in beauty or elegance with her rival.

Concha Douglas is finally impressed by the difference in age between herself and Florestán, some ten or twelve years. She decides to give him up, and does so by an effective lie. She tells him that she and he cannot hope to marry, since she is actually his mother. It takes some time for her to convince Florestán, and even when he begins to accept the idea, he begs her to stay with him. She insists that it is best to separate. At the close of the novel, having decided to return to the United States where she might settle down with Mr. Arbuckle, another suitor, she is portrayed by Blasco as no longer an Amazon queen, but a woman in grief, begging her companion to hide her from the view of passersby. This is in notable contrast with the Mrs. Douglas of the earlier part of the novel, who gives no outward sign of her emotions when she learns that Florestán has been wounded. Then she merely states: "I am not a woman. I do not know how to weep. . . . I have never wept!" (III, 223). Her last words, however, with which the novel closes, are: "I need to weep" (III, 255). Blasco has so carefully prepared for the change with suggestions of the realization of age and maternal emotion that one accepts as credible the transformation, and loses no respect for Mrs. Concha Douglas, the poor Queen Calafia.

CHAPTER 8

The Novels of Spanish Glorification

BLASCO had planned, before the outbreak of World War I, to write a series of novels about Spanish America. Later he decided to return to historical fiction and deal with Spanish celebrities like Pope Benedict XIII, the Borgia family, Christopher Columbus, and Alonso de Ojeda. What was the outcome of these changes in his grand design?

The group that may be termed the novels of Spanish glorification include *El papa del mar (The Pope of the Sea)*, 1925; *A los pies de Venus (At the Feet of Venus)*, 1926; *En busca del Gran Kan (In Search of the Great Khan)*, 1929; and *El Caballero de la Virgen (The Knight of the Virgin)*, 1929. The last two were published posthumously, as was Blasco's final novel, *El fantasma de las alas de oro (The Phantom with Wings of Gold)*, 1930. The transition to this group was made, however, after an experiment in fantasy written by Blasco as a scenario for a motion picture.

I From Gulliver to Benedict XIII

El paraíso de las mujeres (The Paradise of Women), 1922, thus represents a transitional work between the Spanish-American and World War I group and those which re-create Spain in its period of European prestige and expansion. In novels like *Queen Calafia* and *The Land of Everyone*, Blasco drew parallels between historical figures and contemporary women, but the past played a subordinate role. Thereafter he was to plunge deeply into straight historical fiction. Previously, though, he made his excursion into fantasy, in a realm already beloved by readers of English literature.

The setting of *The Paradise of Women* is the land of Lilliput, about which nothing presumably was known after the departure from it of Capt. Lemuel Gulliver, protagonist of Jonathan Swift's *Gulliver's Travels*, first published in 1726. Blasco mentions in the introduction to his novel, dated at Menton in February, 1922, that as a result of the success of the film version of *The Four Horsemen of the Apocalypse* in the previous year, he was asked to write a scenario for another motion picture (II, 1633–37). He goes on to say that the Gulliver story had impressed him as a child and his purpose was to tell what happened in Lilliput since Gulliver's day. The scenario took only three weeks to write, and at the end of that time Blasco found that it had assumed the proportions of a novel.

His choice of setting indicates Blasco's liking for English books. Moreover, the generous role played by the United States in World War I and Blasco's pleasant experiences as a traveler in this country may account in part for the fact that this novel is concerned with Anglo-American rather than with Hispano-American people.

Blasco stated, in an interview toward the end of his life, his belief in a world language, and said that it made little difference to him whether this language would be English or Spanish. He recognized also that the moving picture was, in a sense, a world language, that is, "a universal medium of exchange." [1]

Thus *The Paradise of Women* is a tribute to a great English writer, made to order at the request of representatives of filmdom, and takes the reader from New York City westward toward Australia and the land of the little people. This history of Lilliput is related as part of a dream of the protagonist of the novel, Edwin Gillespie, a young New York engineer. Gillespie has fallen in love with Margaret Heynes, but her mother, Augusta Heynes, does not consider him a suitable match. She had taken Margaret successively from New York to Pasadena, and thence to San Francisco, in an effort to discourage Gillespie's suit. In order to make enough money to become worthy of her daughter's hand, Edwin decides to go to Australia on an English passenger liner. Aboard ship, the dream occurs. Herein is recorded the arrival of the Gentleman-Mountain,[2] Gillespie, to the country near what was known as Van Diemen's Land.[3] Gillespie's ship, as his dream presupposes, had been sunk, perhaps by a floating mine or a torpedo.

The situation in Lilliput is no longer the same; women have assumed control of the government, now known as the United States of Happiness, which includes Lilliput's traditional enemy, the island of Blefuscú, and the capital is the present City-Paradise of Women, the former Mildendo.

Assigned to Gillespie as interpreter is a university professor of English, a woman named Flimnap (the name is derived from Swift), who explains to Gillespie all that has happened in the pygmy land since Gulliver's time. She falls in love with the Gentleman-Mountain, despite the difference in their size and the low status of a male giant in this woman-controlled land. War and liquor have been eradicated, and women now assume the functions and dress of men in the era before what is called by them the True Revolution. One of Gillespie's chief flaws for them is that he wears trousers, taboo for men in recent decades.

Blasco's account of the behavior of the Lilliputians of this new society is entertaining, as well as in keeping with Swift's satirical humor. Twentieth-century America has its feminists; the City-Paradise of Women has its masculinists, hoping for the day of restoration of the old order. Among these is Ra-Ra, a miniature double of Gillespie, who befriends him, and his beloved Popito, a diminutive double of Margaret Heynes. Popito's female father, known as Father of the Masters, whose name is Momaren, looks like Mrs. Augusta Heynes, and is hostile to the love between her daughter (who yearns to be a woman of the old pre-True Revolution days) and Ra-Ra. Blasco's use of masculine words to refer to the modern Lilliputian women, and feminine ones for the men, heightens the unreal and humorous effect of the description, but might be confusing if retained in our summary.

The physical resemblances between Gillespie and Ra-Ra and Mrs. Heynes and Momaren, as well as Margaret and Popito, augment the unity between the pygmy and real worlds, and also suit the dreamlike nature of the narrative. The adventure ends with Gillespie's escape from Lilliput after the death of Popito and the suicide of Ra-Ra, which occur in the course of a revolution by the male pygmies. After Gillespie awakens, he finds himself again a passenger on the English ship bound for Australia. A telegram from Mrs. Heynes asks him to return to the United States because of her daughter's illness, and a note from Margaret reveals that she has feigned illness in order to persuade her mother to permit their marriage. This charming scenario presented technical problems to the moviemakers, so that *The Paradise of Women* has not yet been filmed.

As in *The Paradise of Women,* Blasco's historical novel, *El papa del mar (The Pope of the Sea),* dated at Menton from August to October, 1925, consists of two complementary plots. The main emphasis is the evocation of the life and times of Pedro de Luna (*ca.* 1328–1423/24), who was made cardinal in 1375, and was elected by the cardinals of Avignon in 1394 to become successor of Pope Clement VI. He took the title of Pope Benedict XIII and never yielded his claims to his Roman or Pisan rivals.

II *Two Lovers with Columbus*

Blasco gives an account of the papacy since the time of Pope Clement V (1305–1314) by means of a talk by a twentieth-century Spanish historian, Claudio Borja. Borja (in English or Italian, Borgia) becomes interested romantically in a wealthy Argentinian widow, Rosaura Salcedo de Pineda, whom he first meets as guest of Senator Aristides Bustamante, likewise Spanish, at an Avignon hotel. The relationship between Claudio and Rosaura is analogous with that between Tannhäuser and Venus as portrayed in Wagner's opera; the role of Estela Bustamante, daughter of the senator and long-time sweetheart of Claudio, corresponds to that of Elisabeth. Rosaura's quality as woman is not only reminiscent of Wagner's Venus, but also of Helen of Troy and of Lilith (III, 915). Thereby Blasco links Rosaura to earlier striking woman characters. He suggests, too, a kinship between his Claudio Borja and Goethe's Faust (III, 914).

Most of the historical detail is told by Claudio to Rosaura during his romantic pursuit of her, as he serves as guide in various places associated with the Pope of the Sea. Claudio's intention is to write a book glorifying this Spanish Pope; since childhood he has been interested in the popes from Spain—not only Pedro de Luna, but also Pope Calixtus III (Alonso de Borja) and Pope Alexander VI (Rodrigo Borja), whose family name he bears. The romantic adventure terminates in a farmhouse, where Claudio and Rosaura have taken refuge after a broken steering gear and a rainstorm have prevented them from reaching Castellón. They spend the night together despite Rosaura's reluctance to do so; Claudio promises not to betray her.

Blasco shares Claudio's interest in history, and transmits his enthusiasm unmistakably to the reader as he recounts the peregrinations of Pope Benedict XIII from Avignon, where his palace was for a long time under siege. Blasco describes these wanderings to various places in the western Mediterranean area, until Pedro finally reaches a castle on the peninsula of Peñíscola, an appropriate stronghold for this Pope. Blasco tells us that the Pope's companions there dated their letters *In Arca Noe,* Latin for "In Noah's Ark" (III, 1009). The Pope himself used to point out the similarity between the Church, taking refuge in Peñíscola, and Humanity, taking refuge in Noah's Ark at the time of the Great Flood. The love held by the Pope for the Mediterranean and the importance for him of the sea are often suggested by the author, and justify the title of the novel.

This work has met with varied reactions from critics. A somewhat unsympathetic, but unbiased, appraisal is provided by a review of the English translation, where it is described as "a guidebook novel of the baldest sort," but the writer admits that "the history is done with dash and color" and that the author "narrates the whole story with ease and grace." [4] For this critic, the fictional element is weak. A Spanish reviewer, however, commented on the fact that the average reader finds it difficult to decide what interests him most: the last Pope of the Great Schism, the restlessness of the Argentinian widow, or the confused emotions of good Claudio in Peñíscola. [5]

Unfavorable criticism of *The Pope of the Sea* is directed chiefly against the device of presenting history as part of a fictional and illicit love affair and the confusion arising from the juxtaposition of the fourteenth and fifteenth centuries side by side with the twentieth. In any case, as colorful evocation of history and with its interesting setting, the novel merits esteem.

A footnote to the title of Blasco's next novel, *A los pies de Venus (At the Feet of Venus),* subtitled *Los Borgias (The Borgias),* indicates that this work is a continuation of *The Pope of the Sea* (III, 1043). The novel itself is dated at Menton from June to September, 1926.

The same technique is used to combine two plots, one the continuation of the romance of Claudio Borja, at the feet of his beloved Venus (as implied in the title), Rosaura Salcedo de Pineda. The other is the history of the Borgias in Italy, including the popes of that family.

Since the night at the farmhouse, Claudio and his Venus, Rosaura, have traveled together to various places in western Europe, and have then settled in her villa on the Azure Coast, which represents an enchanted Venusberg for the lovers. Gradually their love affair loses warmth, and Rosaura circulates again in society.

Blasco varies the presentation of the history of the Borgias and the Papal court at Rome by permitting Claudio's uncle and a learned South American to discuss with him certain events in that history. This device adds force to the narrative, since the reader sees that, for all three experts in history, the Borgias represent an unjustly maligned and deservedly significant family in Europe of the fifteenth and early sixteenth centuries. Lucrezia Borgia, in particular, is portrayed as an admirable girl and woman.

The love affair between Rosaura and Claudio comes to an end. Claudio decides that he will marry his old sweetheart, Estela Bustamante, and Rosaura plans to marry a young South American attaché named López Rallo, by whom Claudio was wounded in a duel.

The novel ends with a reference to the discovery of the New World by Christopher Columbus and to the Spanish Pope Alexander VI (Rodrigo Borja), who divided the world between the Spanish and the Portuguese. This reference anticipates the next of Blasco's novels, which deals with Columbus and his first voyage.

In Search of the Great Khan is subtitled *Cristóbal Colón,* the Spanish form of the name of Christopher Columbus. This novel is dated at Menton in 1928; it is an appropriate sequel to the preceding historical novels, and is the first of the two novels dealing with the achievements of Columbus and of Alonso de Ojeda, both of them presented in less detail by Blasco in *The Argonauts.*

Blasco's technique here resembles that of the earlier novels combining pure history with a love story—*The Pope of the Sea* and *At the Feet of Venus*—but differs in that the young lovers, Fernando Cuevas and Lucero Cohen, are depicted as participants with Columbus and Ojeda in the historical events in Spain and the New World which the writer describes. The title of the first of the two novels reminds the reader that Columbus believed that he would be able to reach China and the Great Khan by sailing west from Spain. The main plot deals with the first voyage of Columbus and the events leading up to it. Through involvement in the love story of Fernando, a Christian, and Lucero, a Jewess—who is disguised as a boy throughout the novel to avoid identification—the reader becomes aware of the problems of the Jew in the Spain of that era. Those not accepting baptism were expelled from the Spain of Ferdinand and Isabella in 1492, the year of the conquest by the Spanish Christians of Granada, until then under Moorish rule.

III   *Phantom over Monte Carlo*

Of the historical figures presented in this novel, the most vividly and sympathetically delineated is Martín Alonso Pinzón, commander of the "Pinta," who was most influential in the task of recruiting ships and sailors for the voyage, and whose experience and ability as a naval commander are emphasized in the course of the story. For one critic this book resembles a novelistic biography more than a true novel, and is, in spite of certain weaknesses, effective, so much so as to be considered for Spanish readers the best source available for information about the discovery of the Indies.[6]

At the close of *In Search of the Great Khan* is found Blasco's note to the reader entitled "The mystery of Columbus." In this note Blasco says that he has been studying Columbus since 1910 and has read everything written by the chroniclers of Columbus' period and by the most important modern authors. He points out the difficulty of reconstructing the life of Columbus before 1486, the number of cities that have been mentioned as his birthplace, the problem of his ancestry—Italian, Corsican, Spanish—and the identities of the two corpses which are supposed to be his, one in Seville and one in Santo Domingo. Blasco is convinced that the documents testifying to the existence of a Cristoforo Colombo in Genoa are authentic, but that this Colombo is not to be identified with the explorer. The desire of Columbus to hide his origin has been attributed, the author claims, to vanity or snobbishness, to his having committed acts of piracy, and to his having been a Jew. Columbus was neither a saint nor a learned man but simply, in Blasco's words, "a man of enormous good qualities and great defects, extraordinarily favored by fortune in his first voyage and abused by it in the following ones, who discovered a new world without ever knowing what he had done, the most famous and transcendental mistake presented by human history" (III, 1398).

The sequel to *In Search of the Great Khan,* dated posthumously at Menton in 1929, is *The Knight of the Virgin,* subtitled *Alonso Ojeda,* the name of its chief historical figure.

Ojeda was one of the ship commanders who accompanied Columbus on his second voyage to the New World. Aboard Ojeda's ship as passengers were Fernando Cuevas and his wife, Lucero, described by Blasco as the only lady of legal status to be with the fleet, although there were also some low-class women who went along as companions of the sailors and soldiers. The novel deals with the subsequent voyages of Columbus and of Ojeda, and with events which took place in Spain's New World settlements in the period between 1493 and the death of Ojeda, about 1515.

Blasco contrasts the story of Fernando and Lucero, who gradually become successful as farmers in the New World, with the successes and failures of leaders like Columbus and Ojeda. Through Lucero's words he implies that hard, steady farm work earns more satisfying results than the efforts spent by some in the quest of gold. As she says to Fernando: "Let others go in search of gold. Let us strive for the land to maintain our pigs, our cows, and to give us maize and manioc. Let Don Alonso and those like him seek new mines. We shall sell them the food for their voyages, and God will cause them, in the end, to work for us, without our moving from our home" (III, 1449).

The character of Lucero is marked by shrewdness and courage. She undergoes considerable development in the course of the two novels, and in one striking scene she shows that she is by no means inferior to other Amazons who figure in Blasco's novels. This takes place when Ojeda, who has come to have a strong and non-Platonic affection for her, attacks her with violent passion. She defends herself, first with her husband's sword, and then by biting his face so as to draw blood. Finally she calls the names of Ojeda's respected friend, Juan de la Cosa, and her husband, and frees herself from Ojeda's embrace, as she says to him: "And Your Excellency thinks himself to be a knight? Coming to steal his wife by force from a friend who was always ready to give his life for friendship. . . ! Aren't you ashamed when you think what the Virgin who protects you would say about so base an act?" (III, 1464).

Lucero is successful in restoring Ojeda to his senses; her final appeal to his devotion to the Virgin Mary is apposite, and is one of numerous references to the Mariolatry of the *conquistador,* which provides the novel with its title. Ojeda carries with him a miraculous image of the Virgin (III, 1417).[7] In Spain, Ojeda had left behind a sweetheart, a virgin named Isabel Herboso, who became a nun before her death.[8]

When suffering great hardships in the swamps of Cuba, Ojeda promises the Virgin to erect in her honor a chapel in the first Indian settlement he might reach, and to leave there her image for the pagans to worship, if she would come to his aid (III, 1487–88). He keeps his vow with considerable sorrow, since it means separating himself from the miraculous image. The career of Ojeda closes on a sad note; he dies in poverty, leaving behind him an Indian concubine, baptized with the name of Isabel, and children in Santo Domingo. The friars of a Franciscan church bury him at the door so that all who enter will tread upon his remains (III, 1504).

The novel closes with the death of Ojeda's Indian concubine, who, with her three children, had joined Cuevas and his wife and their son—who was named Alonso after Ojeda, the first Creole born in the New World. A conflict of attitudes or generation gap between Alonso and his parents appears and has a symbolic significance for Blasco. Alonso tells his parents: "I was born in this land, and you came from afar to seize what did not belong to you" (III, 1509). Blasco explains that this attitude represents that of the Creole, or person born in the colonies having European blood, who is beginning to rise against his progenitors. Ojeda's children, *mestizos,* obey their Creole companion better than they do Fernando and Lucero, and when they play together are incited by him against their playmates who were born in Spain. Fernando Cuevas' philosophical statement, which ends this novel, predicts the struggle for independence of Spain's New World colonies:

"What we are doing now may last for centuries, and afterwards will come a day when our children's children will calmly eject us from the house which we built for them at the cost of many sufferings, of so much blood. . ." (III, 1509).

The last novel by Blasco, *El fantasma de las alas de oro (The Phantom with Wings of Gold)*, continues only very indirectly the theme of Spanish glorification, but rather returns to the Riviera, the setting of *The Enemies of Women.* The symbolic title suggests money and, ultimately, death.

The phantom with wings of gold is said to sleep every night in the casino of Monte Carlo and is first mentioned by one of the cosmopolitan habitués of this gambling world, a Russian named Sergio Briansky, whose nickname is "The Boyardo." The phantom is frequently mentioned in the course of the novel. Its wings sound alluringly of the wealth to be gained there, and it presages the fatal summons.

The heroine is a gambler's daughter, Jazmina Tavera, born in Cuba of Spanish parents. She marries a wealthy older man to gain economic security for herself and her parents. Circumstances lead to an illicit love affair between Jazmina and an Argentinian artist, Marcelo Williams Cereceda. Eventually she confesses to her husband the truth and, in spite of his anger at the revelation, they decide to remain man and wife. Six years later, with Monte Carlo changed in many ways as a result of World War I, Jazmina, now widowed, and Marcelo meet again, but he has become engaged. The novel ends with Jazmina's decision to leave Monte Carlo and let Marcelo marry his fiancée, even though Marcelo still loves her.

The Phantom with Wings of Gold reminds the reader of earlier novels by Blasco. It includes a heroine with will power, the evocation of the atmosphere of Monte Carlo and Monaco, a title of symbolic significance reiterated throughout the work, references to World War I, bits of historical and geographical background (e.g., the silver mines of Mexico, the Museum of Oceanography in Monaco), and allusions to music. The book suggests that Blasco's interest in the vein of Spanish glorification had slackened; he was again exploiting the Riviera as setting, and self-sacrifice in love as theme.

CHAPTER 9

Short Stories, Novelettes, and Nonfiction

THOUGH it is by his novels that Blasco Ibáñez achieved his greatest fame, his short fiction and nonfiction writings are important in revealing his development as a writer. Even had he remained only a writer of short stories, he would have been entitled to the sobriquet of the Spanish Maupassant.

Chronologically, the short stories begin with "La torre de Boatella" ("The Boatella Tower"), written in Valencian in 1883. In 1887 appeared his collection *Fantasías, leyendas y tradiciones (Fantasies, Legends, and Traditions)*, in Spanish, with medieval tones, treated largely in the Romantic manner. In the following year appeared another collection of stories, *El adiós de Schubert (Schubert's Farewell)*. Neither of these volumes forms part of the canon recognized by Blasco as worthy of preservation in his collected works. They are in general not characteristic of the more mature author, whose later short stories, like his novels, conform to the tenets of the Realists and Naturalists to a greater degree than to those of the Romanticists, who were by that time somewhat out of fashion.

Cuentos valencianos (Valencian Tales) appeared in 1896, but some of the pieces had been published in Blasco's newspaper, *El Pueblo,* since 1892. This collection contains thirteen stories, including the remarkable one entitled "Dimoni." It tells of a flageolet player named Dimoni ("Demon"), whose alcoholic wife dies giving birth to a deformed fetus. Blasco succeeds in combining rough humor with pathos and sympathy. Dimoni's sorrow is deeper for having known love and despair as a result of his marriage and loss; the emotions are all the more moving, perhaps, in being centered on rustic Valencians portrayed with unflattering realism. "Dimoni" is one of the best examples of Blasco's power in the short story.

I *A Pyre on the Gibraltar Beach*

Realistic or Naturalistic topics like the effects of liquor, the results of adultery, violence, the lives of the Valencian peasants, death, disease, prison life, and cruelty stand out in the collection as a whole. These stories naturally remind the reader of incidents and characters in the Valencian novels. *Reeds and Mud* has points of comparison with "Dimoni," "Cosa de hombres" ("Male Affairs"), and "La cencerrada" ("The Serenade"). The trash collector Nelet of "El 'femater' " ("The Trash Collector") is a character in *Rice and a Carriage* (I, 291).

The death from diphtheria of the child of the lawyer Don Andrés in "La caperuza" ("The Cape") recalls the death of Pascualet from pneumonia in *The Cabin* (I, 534). A somewhat unusual theme is that of "Noche de bodas" ("Wedding Night"), depicting the despair of a priest on the wedding night of the woman he might have married, and who now feels, like Prometheus, condemned to eternal torment.

The collection entitled *La condenada (The Condemned Woman)* appeared in 1900. It is similar in vein to the previous one, and likewise contains several stories published earlier. The title is taken from the brief story of a woman whose husband is in prison under a death sentence. Eventually the sentence is commuted, but when she expects his release she is informed that he will be sent off to Africa. His wife feels that she, now, is condemned, with neither the consolation of being able to live again with her husband nor of being released from her marriage.

Among these stories are some of Blasco's best and most famous. "Primavera triste" ("Sad Spring") contrasts the treacherously beautiful Huerta with the hopeless fate of those who cultivate it, whose strength is sapped by the demands it makes on them.

"El parásito del tren" ("The Parasite of the Train") tells of a man who, too poor to pay for the ticket to ride the train so as to spend Sundays with his family, is forced to board illegally. Thus he is pursued by the Civil Guard and employees of the railway. Eventually the body of this "parasite" is found torn to pieces by the wheels.

"Golpe doble" ("A Shot in the Dark") is a story of extortion and vengeance, with a surprise ending, in which the mayor and constable are discovered to have been the culprits. "Hombre al agua" ("Man in the Water") presents the struggle of Juanillo against drowning and his last thoughts. "El ogro" ("The Ogre") is a humorous characterization of a carter with a rough exterior who shows his good-heartedness by taking back to their feline mother, despite inconvenience and the heat of an August day, five kittens he discovers in his cart.

"La pared" ("The Wall"), last in the collection, is symbolic of the long hatred existing between the Rabosa and the Casporra families, whose houses are separated by this wall. When one of the houses catches fire, old Tío Rabosa is trapped inside. Three young Casporras enter and rescue him, as well as some of the furniture and property, at the cost of a broken leg to one of them. The old man's gratitude leads to friendship between the families and the wall is torn down.

Blasco's novelette *Luna Benamor*, taking its title from the heroine's name, appeared in 1909, soon after his novel *The Dead Command*. The theme of the novelette contrasts with that of the novel, which concerned shifts in attitude between despair and determination, with a final happy relationship. In *Luna Benamor,* the author shows a different outcome for a similar case.

Luis Aguirre is a young Spanish member of the foreign service, awaiting a ship at Gibraltar after having received an appointment as consul to Australia. The cosmopolitan scene at Gibraltar is described through the eyes of Aguirre. He falls in love with a young Jewess, Luna ("Moon") Benamor, granddaughter of an old and successful money changer, whose ancestors were Spanish Jews.

Luna's father was an exporter of Moroccan tapestries in Rabat. There Luna, named Horabuena, was born, the older of two sisters. The younger, named Asibuena, died of a fever after the Moroccans burned their house, and Horabuena and her mother lived in fear of the Moslems, who disliked the Jews. On one occasion, Horabuena's mother sensed the presence of the devil. She feared he would take Horabuena, and in order to deceive him said that Horabuena was not at home, and that the child with her was Luna. Later, the name was formally changed to Luna at the synagogue.

At the time the events at Gibraltar take place, Luna, now bereft of parents as well as sister, is with her grandfather and her uncle Zabulón, his wife Thamar, and their two daughters, Sol ("Sun") and Estrella ("Star"). She has been betrothed since the age of twelve to Isaac Núñez, a Jew whose family lived in Tangiers and who had become successful in Buenos Aires. When Aguirre falls in love with Luna, Blasco takes the opportunity to describe for the reader some of the history, attitudes, and customs of the Spanish Jews.

Aguirre is successful in winning Luna's heart, but her family and traditions oppose the union. Isaac comes to Gibraltar at this time, and Luna bids farewell to Luis, saying that she would always remember this episode as a beautiful dream. Aguirre, recalling the story of Horabuena, tells the pursuing devil that his beloved is not Luna, that she is Unica ("Unique"). Luna says that Aguirre's God is not hers, and turns her back on love. The differences in culture and outlook of the young Spaniard and the Jewess are stressed in part by the device of having

Aguirre gain knowledge from his friend, an Indian bazaar keeper from Madras named Khiamull, an experienced traveler. Khiamull reflects upon the wisdom of the East, and through his statements one glimpses Asian attitudes that may surprise a Western reader.

The unfortunate failure of Aguirre's suit for Luna's hand coincides with Khiamull's admission to the hospital with a cough so bad as to cause hemorrhage. Just after Aguirre has booked passage on a steamer for Port Said, he learns of the death of his Indian friend, and from the ship he sees the fire consuming Khiamull's pyre on the beach at Gibraltar, the wood for which was supplied by the benevolent British government.

Tradition has won a victory over the love of Luis Aguirre and Luna Benamor, but the close of the novelette is gently melancholy rather than tragic. The sorrow felt at the death of wise Khiamull, far from his native Madras, is assuaged by the thought of the survival of his soul in the flight of the seagulls and the roar of the foam, giving the reader new strength to keep on living, in spite of disappointment.

II *Love, a Monopoly of the Rich*

To fill out the *Luna Benamor* volume, Blasco added a miscellany of tales, sketches, and notes. The tales include six pieces. In "Un hallazgo" ("A Find") Magdalena tells how he came to be sentenced to prison while helping a friend to rob a house. He takes, without realizing it, a child along with the mattresses. Softheartedly, because of the resemblance of this "find" to his own child, he returns with it, only to be caught by the police. In "El último león" ("The Last Lion"), the oldest of the tanners, aged Vicente, takes the role of the lion in a festival, in accordance with family tradition. The three-hour procession tires him; he is given ice cream and an almond drink, gets pneumonia, and is buried in the glorious, hairy lion suit. The prostitute Mari-Pepa, in "El lujo" ("Luxury"), having left home with the mayor's son, who deserted her, prefers to keep on with her trade, since she was born to enjoy luxury. Tío Pascual's only son, in "La rabia" ("Rabies"), has been bitten by a dog. Eventually the father is forced to shoot his son, who had already been planning marriage, because of his suffering in the throes of rabies. In "El sapo" ("The Toad"), Visanteta, girl friend of Carafosca, has a mysterious illness; people think she has a toad in her belly. One night the doctor determines that she is pregnant. The people fear that Carafosca may want to kill her, but he loves her even more. In "Compasión" ("Compassion"), a financially ruined noble, Count

Segreda, gambles with his friend the Viscount de la Tremisinière. The viscount, full of compassion, tries to lose. The revelation is too much for the count, who commits suicide because of the shame of having been pitied by his friend.[1]

The sketches and notes in this volume comprise the following five. "El amor y la muerte" ("Love and Death") shows that these two powers are different but accompany each other. Men fear and desire "La vejez" ("Old Age"); it has certain advantages. In "La madre Tierra" ("Mother Earth") Blasco states that man's true family consists of Father Sun, Mother Earth, and Sister Water; progress has come from Mother Earth. "Rosas y ruiseñores" ("Roses and Nightingales") shows the gardens of Aranjuez as full of birds and flowers. Both perfume and music give pleasure. The song of the nightingale is like perfume; he is the rose of the night. "La casa del labrador" ("The Laborer's Cottage") recalls a visit to the cottage built by King Charles IV in 1803 at Aranjuez, where he could play at tilling the soil. Nearby one can sense a Spain that is no longer alive.

A collection entitled *El préstamo de la difunta (The Dead Woman's Loan)* appeared in 1921. The title story is actually long enough to be classed as a novelette. It reflects Blasco's interest in South America. The chief character is a gaucho named Rosalindo Ovejero, from the mountainous northwestern part of Argentina. An unfortunate fight leads him to flee to Chile across the Andes. On the way he reaches the grave of the woman of the title, who had died in that remote region and been buried there with her young son. Wayfarers are accustomed to leave alms at the grave, in order to assure a safe trip. The needy gaucho borrows—as had others before him—a small sum, leaving a receipt with a promise to repay it with interest.

Afterwards, Rosalindo is attended by bad luck, which he attributes to the dead woman's impatience as he sees her in alcohol-induced dreams. He tries to have her money returned with interest by intermediaries, but continues to be haunted. Finally he decided to go to the grave himself. There he is attacked and killed by a giant puma who keeps vigil there. Considerable skill is shown by Blasco in characterization of the unlucky Rosalindo and in description of the hostile environment.

Unforgettable is "El monstruo" ("The Monster"). This story contrasts the reactions of the mother and of the wife of a Maurice Delfour, who had lost both arms, both legs, and one eye in battle in World War I. The wife is repelled, but the mother accepts the "monster" into her loving arms.

Other stories in the collection relating to the same war include "Noche servia" ("Serbian Night"), "Las vírgenes locas" ("The Mad Virgins"), "La vieja del 'cinema' " ("The Old Woman of the Movies"), "Un beso" ("A Kiss"), "La loca de la casa" ("The Madwoman of the House")—in which the "madwoman" is the dementedly overactive imagination of a coward—and "El empleado del coche-cama" ("The Sleeping Car Porter"). South America is again reflected in "Las plumas del caburé" ("The Caburé Feathers")—the *caburé* being a type of owl—and "Los cuatro hijos de Eva" ("The Four Sons of Eve"). The Mexican Revolution, viewed unsympathetically, inspired "El automóvil del general" ("The General's Automobile"), in which Isidro Maltrana reappears, and also "La sublevación de Martínez" ("The Insurrection of Martínez").

Novelas de la costa azul (Stories of the Côte d'Azur) appeared in 1924. Blasco explains in a note to the reader that the title was given because the majority of these six "novelistic stories" and "descriptive narratives" have the Côte d'Azur, along the Mediterranean, as setting. They are actually novelettes. "Puesta del sol" ("Sunset") portrays two people, eighty years old or more, now living separately in the French Riviera, who might have lived happily many years together if the man had only let the woman know, a half century before, that he had fallen in love with her. "La familia del doctor Pedraza" ("Dr. Pedraza's Family") shows a self-sacrificing doctor of Buenos Aires who is run over by a train, presumably to enable his unworthy wife and children to benefit from his life insurance. "El sol de los muertos" ("The Sunshine of the Dead") concerns a famous elderly writer, living in Paris. In love with a woman much younger than he, the writer learns that she is really in love with his young secretary, and decides to withdraw his suit and be their benefactor. "El comediante Fonseca" ("Fonseca the Actor") introduces the reader to a retired Spanish actor in an old folks' home on the Cantabrian coast, who relates his career as an actor in South America. "El viejo del paseo de los ingleses" ("The Old Man of the Promenade des Anglais") is the story of an old Russian nobleman who comes to the realization that love is the monopoly of the rich. "En la Costa Azul" is a series of sketches with the Côte d'Azur as setting.

III   *"Black Legend" and* Don Quijote

Novelas de amor y de muerte (Stories of Love and Death) was published in 1927. One of them, "El despertar del Buda" ("The Awakening of the Buddha"), first published in 1896, was reprinted in this collection with only slight corrections by the author. The others are "El secreto de la baronesa" ("The Secret of the Baroness"), about a noblewoman who kills her illegitimate grandchild by burning it alive; "Piedra de Luna," about a Hollywood actress named Piedra de Luna (Moonstone); "El rey Lear, impresor" ("King Lear, Printer"), about a father resembling Shakespeare's Lear, who resorts to suicide; "La devoradora" ("The Devouring Woman"), about a selfish elderly Russian fortune seeker; and "El réprobo" ("The Reprobate"), about a man who wishes to go to Hell to join his sweetheart there.

A detailed analysis of Blasco's short stories was prepared as a dissertation by John B. Dalbor. He concludes that Blasco's most successful stories are contained in three collections: *Valencian Stories, The Condemned Woman,* and *The Dead Woman's Loan.* He also believes that Blasco was more successful as a writer of short stories than of novels. Certainly it is possible to understand Dalbor's opinion that Blasco's best stories reach the level of those of Maupassant or of Chekhov.[2]

The three volumes of Blasco's collected works include a number of volumes of nonfiction. Earliest of these is *En el país del arte (In the Land of Art),* published in 1896. It contains impressions of his three months in Italy, where he took refuge from Spanish authorities as a result of his sympathy for the Cuban cause. This early book is marked by enthusiasm and vigor. Blasco describes the success of Giordano's opera *Andrea Chénier,* in its first performance, as well as the failure of Mascagni's *Zanetto* (I, 167–68). He praises the works of Edmondo De Amicis, whom he met in Turin, and states that he was an avid reader of this writer's tales even before becoming the admirer of Victor Hugo, Emile Zola, and Alphonse Daudet (I, 175). *In the Land of Art* evokes the artistic and political past of Italy's great cities. Naples, "the true Italy," particularly appeals to Blasco, who finds in this city's people much that is Spanish (I, 207).

Oriente, another work resulting from Blasco's travels, appeared in 1907. This account covers Vichy, Geneva, Berne, Constance, Munich, Vienna, Budapest, the Balkans, and Turkey, with emphasis on the easternmost part of his route. Some of the chapters appeared in newspapers in Madrid, Buenos Aires, and Mexico. Blasco's lively style and interest in music, history, and geography are evident. Munich is characterized as the Athens of Germany, drenched in beer (II, 26). The Wagnerian festival, the blue Danube, the dogs of Constantinople, the Greek Pope who addresses the author as "Blascos Ibañides" and who recalls having seen in Greek translation a play by the Spanish Nobel

Prize winner Echegaray (II, 89), the harems and slave markets—these are some of the topics treated by Blasco in *Oriente.* Yet another travel book, the sumptuous *Argentina y sus grandezas (Argentina and Its Grandeurs),* appeared in 1910, the result of the novelist's tour of Argentina.

Blasco took a trip to Mexico in 1920, in order to obtain material for a projected novel, which was to be entitled *El águila y la serpiente (The Eagle and the Serpent).* During this visit, a revolution broke out against President Carranza. After leaving Mexico, Blasco was interviewed by newspaper reporters in New York City, and he felt that their accounts did not present his ideas and statements accurately. He prepared in Spanish articles discussing the revolution, whose leaders he did not sympathize with, and these were translated into English for publication in American newspapers. Blasco then decided it was his duty to set the record straight and make clear his attitude in opposition to the Mexican generals (see II, 1445—54, especially 1452). The resulting volume, *El militarismo mejicano (Mexican Militarism),* was published in 1921. The chapters are outspoken, and marked by the same style that makes his novels and stories interesting. For example, he describes Pancho Villa as a man who "does not smoke, does not drink, whose weakness is woman . . . the presence of a good female produces on him such a profound effect that immediately his enormous lower jaw falls . . . and a thread of slaver begins to drip down . . . the slaver of emotion" (II, 1502).

Blasco's next travel work appeared in 1924—1925 in three volumes, *La vuelta al mundo de un novelista (A Novelist's Tour of the World).* It describes Blasco's cruise on board the Cunard liner "Franconia" in 1923—1924, between New York City and the Riviera via Cuba, Panama, Hawaii, Japan, Korea, Manchuria, China, Macao, Hong Kong, the Philippines, Java, Singapore, Burma, Calcutta, Ceylon, the Sudan, Nubia, and Egypt. Blasco's interest in history, as well as in people, is as marked in this book as in his others; but the information relayed to his reader is not always accurate, as might be expected of an account of so many different places, some of them visited for only a brief time.

A work of propaganda is Blasco's *Alfonso XIII desenmascarado (Alfonso XIII Unmasked),* published in 1924, in which he attacked Spain's king and the prime minister, Primo de Rivera.

The reactions of distinguished writers to other writers are always of interest. Blasco wrote, between 1918 and 1924, several essays on contemporary writers, particularly French, which were collected under the title of *Estudios literarios (Literary Studies),* published posthumously around 1933. Of equal interest is *Discursos literarios*

(Literary Lectures), which appeared as late as 1966, with an introduction by Blasco's biographer, Emilio Gascó Contell. This collection includes twelve lectures given by the writer during his 1909 tour of Argentina and several others delivered in 1911, 1920, and 1921. These lectures attest to the breadth of Blasco's interests and his love for Spain. They deal with such topics as the "black legend" about Spain, the great Spanish discoverers, Cervantes and *Don Quijote*, mysticism, painting, the modern novel, and two favorite French novelists—Emile Zola and Victor Hugo.

CHAPTER 10

Anatomy of a Career

W HAT have the critics of the world considered to be the stature of
Vicente Blasco Ibáñez? What were his theory of literature,
methods of composition, and stylistic influences? Finally, what has
Blasco to offer the reader in the latter third of the twentieth century?

All his life, Blasco was antiroyalist and antidictator. In his own
country this defiance of authority earned him obloquy, imprisonment,
or silence, and much of his work was done in exile. His followers and
friends were likewise stigmatized and dared show little admiration for
what he wrote. Most of the standard Spanish works of reference ignore
or berate him.[1] Much comment on Blasco's books is motivated merely
by partisan attitudes.[2] Envy reared its head when Blasco compounded
his crimes by becoming a millionaire on the proceeds of his pen.

More recently, however, signs have appeared that eventually Blasco
will be given deeper study and wider credit. The author of a
three-volume study of Blasco, after noting the usual defects, remarks:
"On the other hand, there is no Spaniard anywhere among those of his
generation who with greater enthusiasm and without any official
support has spread around the world the name of Spain and its glories,
constantly refuting the anti-Spanish 'black legend.' "[3]

A typical Spanish critique is given by the anonymous editor of the
Collected Works (I, 13): "In Blasco Ibáñez one may discuss his slight
literary background, his incapacity to deal with the problems of
retrospective vision *à la* Flaubert, his slovenly style, his defects of form
in composition, his lack of proportion in structure. Yes, in the works of
Blasco alternate the hits and misses, vulgarity and originality. But what
must be recognized in him is his prodigious and vivid imagination; his
implicative phraseology, embroidered with lights and tones; his human
power to create characters of flesh and blood; his facility and evocative
grace; his happy, easy, and original literary images; the expansive
tension of the novelist's empathy; his power of illumination, running
through many pages of his best novels; and the allure and urbanity that
hold sway in any chapter of any of his books."

I *The Best Critic is the Public*

After citing some representative Spanish critics, especially of
Blasco's novels, Joaquín de Entrambasaguas concludes: "The impression given by all these judgments is contradictory, but not
indicative of lack of interest in the majority of cases, for in them the
literary figure of Blasco, at times obscured by the human figure, almost
vanishes from us among the yeses and noes. I believe we shall never
capture the true literary—or what is almost the same, novelistic—
creation of Blasco Ibáñez if we do not discriminate among his
productions, the totality of his novels, with regard to times and
circumstances." [4] Certainly it is true that the evolution of our
author—even, to put it baldly, his rise and decline—must be considered.
Discrimination is essential, but literary historians who must pigeonhole
the career of a lifelong author have no space in their books for such
analysis and acumen.

The volumes allowed to be sold in Spain today are not free from
tampering; collation even of the three-volume collected works with the
original editions would reveal the labors of the censor. Abroad, the task
of the serious critic was often hampered by lack of faithful translations.
No reliable critical volume on Blasco, based on a deep study of his life
and milieu, as well as on a chronological rereading of some thirty-five of
his most important books, has hitherto appeared in any language.

A year after Blasco's death, his publishing firm in Valencia issued a
small book of homage, but it contains few tributes by important
contemporaries expressing judgments on his literary merits. [5] The usual
Spanish opinion admires Blasco's adventurous life more than the results
of his labors at the desk. He is often damned by faint praise as a
competent Regionalist or local-colorist.

English-speaking critics have on the whole been more fair to Blasco
than those of his own land. As early as 1919, William Dean Howells
paid tribute to his powers of delineation. [6] Havelock Ellis, an
Englishman, wrote in 1924: "In his life and in his works this son of
indomitable Aragon has displayed all the typical Spanish virility, the
free-ranging personal energy, the passion for independence which of old
filled Saragossa with martyrs and heroes." [7] Walter Starkie, another
Englishman who knew Spain well, praised Blasco's energy and
generosity and concluded, in a sketch soon after the author's death:
"Looking back over his work, we are struck by the vast expanses
covered by his imagination. He was a big, untidy genius with no gift of
style, but sometimes when his imagination ran riot he would dash off

scenes in hot haste that are among the most striking in all the modern literature of Spain." [8] Gerald Brenan, although not a wholehearted Blasco fan, did laud certain of his works. [9]

Scholarly attention has been given, for example, to Blasco's short stories and to the exactitude of his rendering of actual locales; but much useful graduate study could still be devoted to analyses of his works, using current critical techniques. The more useful commentaries on Blasco Ibáñez, from Spanish and English sources, are annotated in the Bibliography of this book.

The conception of the novelist and his function held by Blasco Ibáñez was stated in various places. He firmly believed, for example, that novelists are born, not made, and that the most important quality of the novelist is his individuality. Great novelists are scarce. "It is not enough for a novelist to know the art of writing," he told Dr. Balseiro in Menton. "There are many skilled writers, but few novelists able to arouse the entire world . . . for each hundred writers there are probably only two or three novelists." [10]

The best source of Blasco's opinions on the theory of the novel, on his methods of composition, and on the writers he believed influenced him most strongly has fortunately been preserved. This is a letter written to the Spanish critic Julio Cejador in 1918. These invaluable statements, jotted down when the author was fifty-one, were not controverted by him in his remaining years. The letter, appearing in a volume by Cejador, is reprinted in Blasco's *Collected Works* (I, 14–20). [11] On the function of the novelist, for example, he wrote:

I accept the well-known definition that "the novel is reality seen through a temperament." I also think, like Stendhal, that "a novel is a mirror passing along a road." But it is clear that the temperament modifies reality and that the mirror does not reproduce things with their material hardness, for it gives to the image that light, azure fluidity that seems to swim in the bottom of Venetian glasses. The novelist reproduces reality in his manner, suited to his temperament, selecting from that reality what is salient, and rejecting, as useless, the mediocre and the monotonous. . . . Between the reality and the work that reproduces this reality lies a luminous prism that distorts things, concentrating their essence, their souls, exaggerating them: the temperament of the author. For me, the important quality in a novelist is his temperament, his personality, his *special* and *particular* mode of seeing life. This is truly the novelist's style, even if he writes carelessly. And as temperaments are greatly varied (fortunately for art, which dislikes monotony and repetition), thus I do not put great faith in classifications, schools, and categories of certain types of criticism.

Anyone who is truly a novelist is himself and only himself. He probably has a distant relationship with other novelists, but he does not form a close family tie with them. (I, 14)

Later, after decrying the kind of novelist who explains what his intentions are in prologues, manifestos, or books on aesthetics and comparing them to the artist who wrote under a painting, "This is a rooster," Blasco reverts to his theory of the novel, distinguishes between the duties of the novelist and of the critic, and considers the public the best critic of all.

Motion demonstrates itself by walking, and the novelist should demonstrate that he is one by writing novels, only novels. That is what the public wants from him. Then criticism has the task of discerning his intentions, and if the critic is blind and lazy, the public, the great public, with its crowd instinct, will know how to "sense" (even though it does not see it) what exists within the work. In the same way that religions always will count on the gratitude of the faithful, who have received from them consolation and hope, the novels that *are* novels, which vibrate a chord of life and bestow hours of illusion, will be loved by thousands and thousands of readers, even though the critics insist on showing that they are worthless. Criticism appeals to reason, and the work of art appeals to sentiment, to everything in us that forms the world of the unconscious, the world of sensibility, the broadest and most mysterious world we carry within us, since no one knows its limits even remotely, whereas reason is limited. (I, 16)

In evaluating a work, Blasco clearly distrusts the opinion of its author and of most critics, but, it seems, trusts the loving public, all of whose appreciations may be good and who may find values unintended by the author. "The public will clearly see what he has sought to express on his canvas," he continues, "and how he wishes to express it. And if the public gives a dozen different versions, who knows if the definitive one, the one that triumphs, is not better than the one the artist intended? Let us remember that our great Don Miguel in *Don Quijote* perhaps only wished to say one thing, and later the admiration of the whole world has made him say many other things, varied and beautiful."

II   *A Compulsion to Create*

Blasco concludes his letter to Cejador by reverting to his theory of the novel, and states proudly his Platonic ideal of artistic creation as primarily the utterance of the subconscious. This ancient theory is still held by some writers, and has seldom been more clearly expressed.

The important thing is to see objects closely and directly, to live them, if only for a little while, to divine how the rest live. I, dear Cejador, do not believe that novels are created by reason, by intelligence. Reason and intelligence participate in a work of art as directors and arrangers. Perhaps they do not even direct or arrange, remaining on the sidelines of the job as simple advisers. The true and unique constructor is instinct, the subconscious, the mysterious and invisible forces that the ordinary masses label "inspiration." A true artist does things the right way because, being himself, he cannot do them in any other way. The most commendable things in a novel are almost always those of which the author is unaware, and only comes to recognize when the critics point them out. I, when I finish a book, remain as if I had just come out of a dream. I do not know if I have done something worthwhile, or if I have done something stupid. I can't answer questions. I know nothing. . . . The artist who creates beauty is the most unconscious of all producers. This is nothing new. It is a truth as old as the earth. Plato, speaking of poets, said that they utter the most beautiful things without being aware why they say them, and many times without knowing that they have said them. The common people make this same point in the proverb, *El poeta nace, y no se hace:* The poet is born, not made. Reason, intelligence, and reading may shape great writers, inimitable writers worthy of admiration. But they will never become, merely with these elements, novelists, dramatists, or poets. To achieve this, the participation of the subconscious is necessary as the principal factor: the mysterious divination, presentiments, the affective elements, which are, most often, diametrically opposed to the intellectual elements. Clearly we must not abuse this theory, using the sovereignty exercised by the subconscious in a work of art as an excuse, and dispense with reason and study. (I, 20)

Thus Blasco rules out the recent school of automatic creation, which believes that anything they put on paper will be accepted as literature. He does not rule out conscious control.

Everything must harmonize and be used to advantage. Nor can one allow himself, on the pretext that he is dragged along by unconscious forces, to be nonsensical or to blunder. I have said that the unconscious forces are the true workers; but reason gives counsel (if it does not direct), and its presence is always necessary. Finally, dear friend, there is a platitude which, nevertheless, is worthy of pondering: "To write novels, one has to be a born novelist." And to be a born novelist is to bear within himself an *instinct* which enables him to divine the souls of things, to seize upon the salient detail that evokes the proper image, to possess the power of suggestion required for the reader to accept as reality what is a work of pure fancy. He who does not possess this power, however great his talent and his erudition, may write an interesting book, correct and even lovely, when he attempts to write a novel; but he will never write a novel. *(ibid.)*

Blasco's theory of the novel suggests strongly his method of composing fiction. Ample testimony is found, in the Cejador letter and in other places, that Blasco considered himself a born writer, even a compulsive writer, whose subjects changed with his various surroundings.

I write novels because for me this is a necessity. Perhaps I was born to do this, and anything I do to rid myself of this servitude will be useless. There are some who write novels because others have previously written them. Had not a series of models appeared before, they never would have thought ot taking up this work. Had I been born in a savage land, without books, without writings, I am sure I would have journeyed for days to narrate to another person the stories that it would occur to me to imagine in solitude, and beg him, in his turn, to tell me his. Each time I finish a novel I let out a bellow of relief and respite, as if recovered from a painful operation. At last! This is the final one! And I mean it; I am a man of action who has done more in his life than write books, and I do not enjoy sitting for three months with my chest against a desk, writing ten hours a day.... Most of the time, I would choose to live real novels rather than to write them on paper. But each new novel impresses itself upon me with a physiological force, overcoming my tendency to action and my horror of sedentary labor. It grows in my imagination; from a fetus it develops into an infant, it moves, it stands on its feet, beats at my forehead from within, and I have to throw it into the world like a newborn child, under threat of dying, poisoned by the putrefaction of darkness. All that I have said about not working any more is useless. I am convinced that, as long as I am alive, I shall create novels. (I, 16—17)

This prediction became literally true.

"Novels grow like snowballs," he continues.

A sensation and an idea, unsought, risen from the limbos of the subconscious, serve as nuclei, and around them accrete new observations and sensations stored in this same subconscious, without one's being aware of them. The true novelist has an imagination something like a camera, with its shutter forever open. With the same detachment as the camera, without noticing, it collects, during daily life, faces, gestures, ideas, sensations, retaining them unknowingly. Later, slowly, all this wealth of observation is agitated in the mysterious unconscious, amalgamates, crystallizes, awaiting the moment of manifestation; and the novelist, writing under the influence of an invisible force, believes he is uttering newborn thoughts, when he is doing nothing more than transcribing ideas which for years have dwelt inside him and which were aroused by a forgotten person, by a remote landscape, by an unremembered book. I am proud to be a writer as little literary as possible—I mean the least professional. I abhor those who talk at all hours of their profession and are always gathering with colleagues, and cannot exist without them, perhaps because they sustain their lives by gnawing at them. I am a man who *lives,* and moreover, when time permits, writes, from an imperious mental need. Being thus, I believe I am following the noble and manly Spanish tradition. The greatest literary geniuses of our race were men, real men, in the broadest sense of the word: they were soldiers, great travelers, they ventured beyond Spain, suffered captivities and misfortunes—and, moreover, wrote. When they had to battle hand to hand with life, they dropped the pen, considering literary production incompatible with the demands of action. Remember that our Don Miguel [Cervantes] once went for eight years without writing. Thus one gets to know life, I believe, better than by spending one's time in cafes, viewing everything through books or conversations, meeting always the same talkers; mummifying thought with the same affirmations, drinking one's own juices; without seeing other horizons; without moving from the bank near which glides the current of active humanity. (I, 17—18)

Later in the Cejador letter, Blasco underscores even more heavily the effect of environment upon the choice of subject of a novelist.

In writers such as myself—travelers, men of action and movement—the work is the product of the surroundings. Again I recall "the mirror" of Stendhal, an image appropriate to a great artist, connoisseur of life, who also was a traveler and man of action. We reflect what we see. The virtue lies in knowing *how* to reflect. I produce my novels according to the environment in which I live, and have changed my literary face according to the changes in my surroundings, although I am always the same. At this time I am surrounded by an international world, a world of happy idlers, who haunt the choicest parts of the earth in search of pleasure. I study from close at hand grand dukes, princes, and princesses, all the bohemians of royal blood that wander through Europe. I shall depict this world of millionaires and lucky ones, broken and disoriented by the great world catastrophe of the War. Perhaps tomorrow I will live among starving ones, among warriors lost in the solitudes of virgin America, and I shall describe them as well. (I, 19—20)

In short, Blasco wrote because he could not help writing. If further evidence of his *furor scribendi* were needed, it could be found in his reply to a question from his friend Eduardo Zamacois, inquiring whether Blasco thought he had a ready imagination. "Intensely," answered Blasco. "I am impressionistic and intuitive, so that the terrible battle between matter and manner, which other authors so greatly lament, scarcely exists for me. It is a question of temperament. I believe that works of art are conceived instantaneously or never; if the first, the idea grips my imagination with such force and absorbs and possesses me so absolutely that, in order to rest, I have to put it on paper at one stroke. The nervous agitation produced in me by putting into words the final chapters, in particular, constitutes for me a real illness; my hand and breast ache, my eyes ache, my stomach, but nevertheless I cannot stop writing." [12]

III *I Need Only First Impressions*

This conversation also illuminates Blasco's method of handling the novelist's task.

The method he uses in the composition and development of his novels is very simple: at the beginning he has only the main plot, the "block" [of stone], and the names of three or four main characters; the series of episodes, the secondary characters—which we might term "stuffing"— the chapter divisions, etc., come surging along in the ardent flight of his pen. He writes with astonishing celerity and puts into the action whatever occurs to him, so that, when finished, each book is a sort of forest, munificent and wide-spreading. Then comes the "pruning"; the exuberant novelist is eclipsed and the grim critic appears, who cuts, rends, and uproots without pity. [13]

Too often, however, especially in Blasco's later books, the critic is far from grim and the selvas and pampas extend unbounded.

Blasco believed that an obtrusive style tended to shatter the enchantment of a good narrative.

It is wrong to think that the greatest compliment a reader can give a novelist is to exclaim in the middle of his reading: "Heavens, how well this author writes!" The most important quality of the novelist consists in making the reader forget the writer's role as intermediary between him and the story. I greatly appreciate style; but, in the novel, I relegate it to a secondary role. . . . The novelist should think above all about the simplicity and clarity of his work, about the lives of his characters, and about the environment in which these move.[14]

An essay on Blasco's style, after quoting Buffon's dictum that the style is the man, proclaims: "It has been said that the style of Blasco Ibáñez is unequal. If we carried out a detailed analysis of the succession of elements that make up the novels, we would notice those ups and downs; but that which unifies his style—characteristic and unmistakable—is a dynamic power of impatience that makes the words vibrate." [15]

Professor Entrambasaguas decides that structure is the overwhelming component of Blasco's writing: "This is probably the essential characteristic of Blasco's novels: their literary structure; the extremely successful adaptation of all the elements that integrate the novel, giving it a cohesion and unity seldom found. The argument develops into an action, not only graduated perfectly in its emotional force, but in its rising interest; the proportions of dialogue, description, and author's commentary are exact. When one finishes reading one of the better novels of Blasco Ibáñez, he has closed a perfect curve equidistant between all the elements that integrate it and the thought that engendered it." [16]

What were the chief influences of other writers upon the works of Blasco Ibáñez? A number of them have previously been mentioned, such as the possible influence of D'Annunzio on *Among the Orange Trees,* the use of Flaubert's *Salammbô* as an inspiration for *Sónnica the Courtesan,* or the effect upon Blasco's earliest novels of his reading of Zola.

Blasco in the Cejador letter frankly admits the obvious fact that no one escapes the influence of his elders, and that in their beginnings all writers undergo the pressure of tradition, or at least the spell of those authors they see enjoying acclaim. He makes no mention of the fact that the first influence upon his writing was that of an outmoded cloak-and-sword romancer, Fernández y González, and that he began his career in his teens by turning out a dozen volumes of dashing potboilers in order to keep from starving. Blasco later desired that these juvenilia be forgotten, but the critic cannot forget that such an influence might have more effect than one can easily assess. In some of the later novels, where plots flow in a stream of intrigue more reminiscent of Dumas than of Zola, the ghost of Fernández shows its hand more than once. When Blasco lapsed—and his method of composition, dependent as it was upon instinct and inspiration, was likely to cause him to lapse badly when instinct failed—his errors usually lay in the direction of melodrama, coincidence, extravagance, bathos, and mushy love interest; in short, the defects not of naturalism but of cheap historical romance.

Blasco referred to *Rice and a Carriage* as his "first novel" and admitted the effect of Zola upon it, but he felt that soon thereafter he began to break away from Zola's Naturalism, then at the height of its triumph, and to become more and more individualistic.

Perforce I had to begin by imitating someone, as does everyone else, and I am glad that my model was Zola instead of some other anodyne. . . . In our country, which is one of intellectual sloth, the worst that can happen to an artist is to be pigeonholed and labeled—even though gloriously—at the beginning of his career. When I published my first novels, they were found to be similar to the work of Zola, and I was classified forever. This is convenient: thus there exists no future obligation to think or inquire. I, in the eyes of many, no matter what I write, even though I undergo in my literary career the most radical evolution, will always be "the Spanish Zola." Those who say and repeat this with lazy automatism reveal that they do not know Zola or me, or at least, if they know the works of both, have read them hastily, without comprehension. I admire Zola, envy many of his pages, would like to be proprietor of the splendorous oases he opens in the monotonous and interminable desert of the major part of his work; I should be proud to be the author of the crowd descriptions in *Germinal* and the description of the garden in *Paradou;* but, despite this admiration, I recognize that now, in full maturity, when my personality is formed, there remain very few points of contact with my old idol. Zola supported all his work exaggeratedly on a scientific theory, that of physiological inheritance, and this theory, overthrown in part, has reversed the most serious affirmations of his intellectual labor, all the internal framework of his novels. At present, however much I look, I find very few relations with the one alleged to be my literary parent. Neither in the method of composition nor in style de we have the least resemblance. Zola was a reflective writer, and I am an impulsive one. He arrived at his final effect slowly, by drilling. I proceed by explosion, violently and noisily. He used to write a novel a year, patiently, with slow and even progress, like that of a plow; I carry a novel in my head a long time (often two or three of them); but when the moment arrives to put it on paper, a fever of activity seizes me, I lead an existence that could be termed subconscious, and write the book in the time it would take an ordinary copyist to transcribe it. (I, 15)

Despite the very high tribute that Blasco pays to Zola and his admission that at least the Valencian novels were influenced by his example, other differences between the two can be noted than the ones just given by the so-called disciple. The generalizations of Angel del Río—"Blasco Ibáñez is perhaps the only [Spanish] novelist accepting Naturalism in its entirety, with all its artistic and idealogical consequences"[17] and, "He does not have any of the characteristics of twentieth-century literature. . . . Blasco Ibáñez remained a Naturalist with the nineteenth-century social ideology"[18]—are far off the track. By the usual standards of Naturalism—a movement which, by the way, is very much alive in the twentieth century, especially in America, where there have been many practitioners of a modified Zolaism—Blasco was far from being a card-carrying member of this important school.

One criterion of Naturalism, for instance, is scientific objectivity. "We Naturalists, we men of science" said Zola, referring to his followers, who sought to exchange the soap box for the laboratory stool. Blasco, although apparently taking slices of life at random and letting the story tell itself, was actually a special pleader from the start, and as a born storyteller could not maintain the stance of the scientist for a moment. He was, actually, accused of a lax impressionism. He did not take exhaustive notes even for novels that strike one as almost documentary; the surviving notes are sketchy indeed, and far from the sociological accumulations of those who wish to use fiction to serve as unemotional treatises. Blasco once said to Miguel de Unamuno, who wanted him to prolong his stay at Salamanca: "If I look too long I get confused: I need only first impressions."[19]

IV   *Zola, Cervantes, Hugo, and Galdós*

The frankness and amorality one expects of the Naturalist are frequently found in Blasco's novels, and he probes the "lower depths" without prudishness or avoidance of the dirt, the misery, and the horror. But the theory of Naturalism required its practitioners to hold to a philosophy of pessimistic determinism. Blasco was far from being a pessimist. True, he assumed that in the long run the human race would not triumph. But he was constitutionally an optimist to the end, vigorous in body and enthusiastic in spirit. Nor did he feel that all outcomes were predetermined by a god or the fates. He was a reformer, and anyone that tries to remodel his environment is certainly not a determinist who feels that the human will is helpless to modify a preordained outcome. Most of all, Blasco differs from the simon-pure Naturalist in the choice of characters to enact his theme. The endings of many of his novels show the downfall of the protagonist; but the cause is not usually weakness or lack of free will. Moral flaws are not necessarily hereditary. If the character is broken, the blame rests upon social pressures or circumstance. Sometimes, despite the most tragic pressures, the character does not break, and a moral triumph is gained. Batiste in *The Cabin* is as strong at the end as at the beginning, and when the pressure becomes unbearable in the narrow-minded village, he survives to go elsewhere, presumably to carry on the fight to live.

If Zola was not Blasco's lifetime master, where can one look for others? Blasco himself gives some cues. He pays tribute, of course, to Miguel Cervantes; as he wrote to Cejador, "My model, my great man, is Cervantes." Elsewhere he says in the same letter: "Another author has influenced me more powerfully, and no one has noticed: Victor Hugo, with his poetic novels. I tell you that my greatest literary admiration is for Victor Hugo. I do not admire him: I worship him. In my house in Paris I have his portrait and bust in every room, even in the dining room" (I, 18). And in the moment before his death, Blasco thought he saw Hugo appear, and bade him enter the door.

Blasco did not expand upon the resemblances with Hugo, but Balseiro has noted a few. Both carried on public campaigns on the side of the left, and both were political exiles. Both were powerful orators. Both loved the sea and wrote about it. Both carried on a war against what Hugo called the "three fatalities of religion, society, and nature." And both had a broad streak of romanticism and poetry in their prose which elevated it at its best above the pedestrian stretches of Balzac and Zola. Both were fond of music, especially that of Beethoven. Further examination would show more specific similarities: the Waterloo scenes of *Les Misérables* are rivaled by the description in *The Four Horsemen of the Apocalypse* of the Battle of the Marne; and there are similarities between *Toilers of the Sea* and *The Mayflower*. Should one want an obvious literary godfather for Blasco, he need look no further than Victor Hugo.

Other influences have been suggested. "He showed a determined desire to establish in Spain the realistic genre of Zola and Maupassant united with the symbolism of Ibsen and Maeterlinck" is the dictum of the standard Spanish encyclopedia.[20] A similar tack is taken by another reference work: "When he combined the influence of Zola and Maupassant with that of the great school of Spanish *costumbrismo* and *regionalismo,* his dynamic, colorful style produced masterpieces." [21]

A notable lack so far in the list of possible influences is the name of any Spanish writer except Cervantes. Blasco's admiration for the author of *Don Quijote* was great, but such a distant influence on style or material would be hard to demonstrate in detail. Blasco's volume of *Literary Studies,* containing essays of appreciation on thirty-one authors, does not include a single Spaniard. It is generally agreed that he looked abroad for his literary idols, rather than to the café-haunting novelists of Madrid. There was a notable coolness between Blasco and "Azorín," even though the latter was one of the wild young men who had made *El Pueblo* a lively newspaper.

The Spanish novelist most comparable to Blasco Ibáñez is Benito Pérez Galdós (1843–1920). Dr. Balseiro considers the example of Galdós as probably having the greatest effect upon Blasco's novels.

Galdós, who published his first novel in the year of Blasco's birth, started in 1881 with *La desheredada* his series of reformist novels on social themes, using the methods of Naturalism. He was influenced in literature mainly by Dickens, Balzac, Zola, and Cervantes, and his theories of history and life were early based on those of Hippolyte Taine and Auguste Comte (both determinists) and later G. W. F. Hegel and Arthur Schopenhauer (neither of whom was an optimist).

A brief comparison of the lives of Galdós and Blasco shows many marked similarities between these two men a generation apart. Both grew up in distant provinces until they escaped to Madrid. Both were precocious writers and voracious readers, and both had keen powers of observation and memory. Both were indifferent students at the university, but both completed degrees in law. Both went early to Paris and were influenced by cosmopolitan ideas, later traveling widely in Spain and abroad. Both liked music. Galdós and Blasco were even fellow deputies in the Cortes; in 1907 the former returned to politics and became chief of the coalition between the republican and socialist forces. Both, however, found their salvation in writing voluminously, and both preferred to contemplate reality rather than to escape into illusion. Although their personal relationship was not close, it was Galdós who presided in 1900 at the dinner of homage in Madrid that marked Blasco's arrival as an important novelist. The fact that Galdós "took part in the political battle against the Church (as a political institution) and the clergy (as citizens of the state)" [22] might have had more than a slight effect on the writing by Blasco of such books as *The*

Cathedral. The most marked similarity is, of course, the devotion of both to revealing Spanish history in lengthy cycles of novels—Galdós in the many-volumed *Episodios nacionales* begun in 1873, and Blasco in the half-dozen books on Spanish and Spanish-American heroes and heroines beginning in 1901 with *Sónnica the Courtesan* and continuing almost to his last days with the posthumous volumes on Christopher Columbus and Alonso de Ojeda. Certainly the possibility that the example of Galdós was a strong influence on Blasco should not be overlooked.

V *Themes That Will Endure*

In summary, what are the outstanding qualities of Blasco Ibáñez that make him still attractive to the reader in the latter part of the twentieth century?

Born more than a century ago, Blasco the man still offers many attractions to our generation. He was primarily a man, and secondarily a writer. His life was a European success story. Growing up in a family near the edge of poverty, he physically and mentally fought his way for sixty vigorous years. A rebel by choice, a battling newspaper editor, he became embroiled in national politics on the side of the peasants, the fishermen, the slum dwellers, the ignorant, the superstitious. A magnificent orator, he used his rhetoric so violently that the establishment tried to silence him by prison and exile. Spending much of his life outside his native land, he nevertheless remained loyal to the Spanish tradition, seeking to glorify its imperial past and to counteract the anti-Spanish legend. Almost by accident he became a millionaire, and in his will left his villa on the Riviera as a haven for other writers of the world. His body was brought back in triumph to his native city, but even in its streets no monuments remain to his international fame. More paradoxically, Blasco Ibáñez is better known in many other countries than in the Spain whose milieu and people he preserved in his books.

Blasco's most convincing male character was based on his own nature.[23] His main personal trait was a dynamic robustness that forms part of his art. He was a conquistador in literature. His enterprise enabled him to make capital of nearly every experience, happy or painful. Brought up in middle-class surroundings, he portrayed the Valencian bourgeoisie. Living in a seaport, he wrote about the Mediterranean. Imprisoned, he wrote about prisoners. Visiting various Spanish provinces, he wrote about their outstanding problems. His interests spread from art, the Church, and bullfighting to the colonization of America and world wars; his heroes became Spanish popes, soldiers, and discoverers. Despite charges that he was Frenchified or too cosmopolitan, he was always Spanish to his vibrant core. Despising the precious litterateurs of the Madrid cafés, he put his trust in the untutored appreciation of his work by the mass reading public.

Much of Blasco's work is still timely. For example, the motion picture of *The Four Horsemen of the Apocalypse,* filmed in 1921 and dealing with World War I, was remade in 1962 with a setting of World War II, a quarter of a century later, and few changes were needed in the scenario.

Blasco's ideals were high. Far from being a withdrawn Naturalist, objectively reporting on random slices of life, he violently championed many causes that are still alive today. Blasco enlarged his provincial vision until it became a cosmic view. His original mind and gifted imagination were employed in a titanic effort to spread widely his learning, through translating and publishing the works of European thinkers of various countries and philosophies. Like H. G. Wells, the British author whom he resembles in several ways, he embraced the task of becoming a one-man institute of adult education. His sympathy was always with the underdog, but he could portray with compassion the men and women he saw in all strata of society. He was a lover of Mediterranean culture from classical to current epochs, and this background enabled him to expand his scope and become a reliable commentator on Atlantic and American culture as well. His readers around the globe craved such an international view, and he was the most widely translated of all modern Spanish writers.

Blasco's literary qualities have been scrutinized at some length in previous chapters. Briefly, he was a tireless journalist and a magnificent storyteller. From his youth he prolifically poured forth books. His works are the most voluminous in contemporary European literature. Naturally, his product is highly uneven—hence the need for selectivity by the qualified critic. Blasco's fiction covers a boundless range of interests, and his evolution is worthy of scholarly concern. Early stereotyped as a Naturalist of the Zola persuasion, he wrote some of the most impassioned and poignant passages in Spanish fiction. Disdaining "style" as a distraction from the story, Blasco had more than a touch of the poet, and at times his pages are redolent with perfumes and pictorial with images of almost painful beauty. He likewise became one of the masters of Spanish historical fiction, glorifying his country's past. His descriptions of places, impressionistic but precise, have drawn visitors from abroad to view landscapes and edifices he has immortalized (for many people, the province of Valencia will always be Blasco's Valencia). His novels of then contemporary life have become, with the passage of time, valuable sources of social history.

Blasco had a firm theory of the novelist's function, as he explained more than once. He was a craftsman, and his novels often were built on more firm structures than the casual reviewer could perceive. His inborn aesthetic sensibility was sharpened by the need to impress his ideas upon his chosen, broad audience. Working from live models, he created characters who could love and weep and bleed. His ability to depict women is especially notable; they are seldom pretty puppets, and more often vigorous, even masculine, figures dominating their menfolk and impressing their wills on families and even nations.

Observation of Blasco's apparently hasty method of composition led some critics to assume that he carelessly tossed off his masterpieces and rushed into print. Usually, however, the novel composed itself in his mind over a long period, and when the time of parturition came he plunged into a feverish transcription of his pondered prose.

It is possible that, when success showered on Blasco after the whirlwind sales of the English translation of *The Four Horsemen of the Apocalypse,* his work declined in strength as he led the distracting life of a Riviera celebrity. It would be an error, however, to parrot the usual comment that only the Valencian novels are worthy of serious study. The readers of the world will not soon neglect *The Wine Cellar, The Naked Maja, Blood and Sand, The Dead Command,* or *Mare Nostrum.* The five historical novels of Spanish glorification, to which Blasco devoted the energies of his later years, crowned a career. Ramón Menéndez Pidal lauded "above all those final novels, in which he realized a patriotic task worthy of the greatest praise." [24]

Finally, Blasco's themes were often expressed so vigorously that they verged upon propaganda. Yet many of his ideas are still fresh today. Until our generation, or the next one, solves the problems of love, hate, war, race, poverty, art, politics, religion, the dead hand of tradition, colonization, feminism, imperialism, and national loyalties, we should open our minds to the vision of human life found in the fascinating fiction of Vicente Blasco Ibáñez.

Notes and References

Chapter One

1. "Pigmalión," *Blasco Ibáñez, novelista* (Valencia, 1963), p. 42. A useful, brief, but not always factual autobiography may be found in Blasco's *Obras completas,* I, 9–12. All translations in the text of this book are our own.

2. The shop was in the house at No. 8, Calle Nueva Jabonería (the street was later changed to Flor de Mayo) at the corner of Calle de los Angeles. After the capture of Valencia by the Franco troops in 1939, the memorial plaque was removed. The house and the street were later destroyed to make room for the extension of a new Valencia boulevard.

3. Blasco is quoted as saying that the certificate was in error, and that his parents had told him he was born on Sunday the 27th ("Pigmalión," p. 17). Monday was a holiday, and the clerk probably entered the Tuesday date when the certificate was written.

4. The birth certificate, No. 314 in the Archivo Municipal of Valencia, contains other errors. Calatayud is actually in the province of Zaragoza, not Teruel. It gives the father's profession as *cocinero* or cook, but he was proprietor of a small corner grocery. The paternal grandparents were Ramón Blasco and Encarnación Teruel, both of Aguilar; the maternal grandparents were Francisco Ibáñez and Vicenta Martínez, both of Calatayud. The novelist once said that he might have a touch of Moorish blood, a likely possibility in a province that was a battleground of Arabs and Christians for seven centuries.

5. "Pigmalión," p. 18. As examples of the father's lack of sensitivity, this friend of the family says that Gaspar gave his grandchildren pocket knives as presents, and wanted to shoot off dangerous fireworks at their seaside home.

6. These were turned out to earn a living and to obtain money on which to get married. Later Blasco spoke of *Arroz y tartana* (1894) as his "first novel."

7. A visit to the University of Valencia revealed few traces of their most famous alumnus. Only half a dozen of his books were in the library.

8. *Discurso de Blasco Ibáñez pronunciado en una sesión masónica el 3 de Diciembre de 1888* (Valencia, 1888). pp. 4–5, 8.

9. She bore him five children before her death in 1925. The first, born in October, 1892, was an infant girl, named Libertad, who died after three days. Mario, the eldest son, was born on November 9, 1893; he died in 1962, leaving his library, containing some rare editions of his father's works, to the Museo Nacional de Cerámica in the palace of the Marqués de Dos Aguas in Valencia. A second girl was born on March 25, 1895, and was also named Libertad; she married a journalist, Fernando Llorca, and later lived in Mexico. On July 13, 1896, the second son, Julio César, was born; he died in 1919. The third son, Sigfrido, born on July 18, 1902, was still living with his stepmother on Calle General Cantos in Santiago, Chile, in 1964. Blasco's first wife María, as well as his sons Mario and Julio César, are buried in the wall of the Civil Cemetery of Valencia, not far from the vault of the author. A son of Sigfrido, Vicente Blasco-Ibáñez Tortosa, a lawyer, was living in Valencia in 1964. To ensure that he would escape the ill effects of having an atheistic grandfather, this descendant was taken for baptism three times, unknown to each other, by his grandmother, his mother, and a nursemaid.

10. Emilio Gascó Contell, *Genio y figura de Vicente Blasco Ibáñez* (Madrid, 1957), p. 49.

11. José Padín, "Vicente Blasco Ibáñez," lecture at New York Public Library, 1928.

12. José A. Balseiro, *Vicente Blasco Ibáñez, hombre de acción y de letras* (San Juan, Puerto Rico, 1935), p. 18.

13. Gascó, p. 13.

14. "Pigmalión," p. 45.

15. Introduction to *Flor de mayo,* in *Obras completas,* I, 395.

16. In special issue of *La Esfera,* Madrid, 1928.

17. At his beach home of La Malvarrosa, Blasco proudly displayed an American pianola and diverted himself by pedaling out the "Moonlight Sonata" and the overture to "Leonora" ("Pigmalión," p. 86).

18. "Pigmalión," pp. 22, 26, 30, supplies some descriptions of La Malvarrosa when first built; and photographs still exist from that period to confirm his report. The house was of three floors and faced the sea and the beach. Entering through a spacious garden, one found on the main floor a room pretentiously fitted up in Japanese style, a music room, and a bedroom with a telephone nearby. On this same floor was Blasco's personal library and a balcony overlooking the garden. On the next floor above were a reception room, bedrooms, a kitchen and dining room, and a room through which one entered an outdoor portico in Pompeian style with undraped caryatides supporting each of the two corners. This gallery overlooking the sea was the favorite

gathering place of the author and his family. On the top floor was the writing room, with an adjoining photographic darkroom, and several bedrooms. The well-lighted studio, also facing the Mediterranean, was the place where some of the earliest novels were written. An inspection of La Malvarrosa in 1964 showed it to be vacant and in a ruinous condition.

Chapter Two

1. Emilio Gascó Contell, *Genio y figura de Vicente Blasco Ibáñez* (Madrid, 1957), p. 69.

2. Eduardo Zamacois, *Mis contemporáneos* (Madrid, 1910), I, 6–7.

3. Gascó, pp. 107–9.

4. *Ibid.*, pp. 110–11.

5. A partial list of films based on Blasco novels includes the following: *Sangre y arena* (made in Spain with Alcaide and Matilde Domenec), 1916; *The Four Horsemen of the Apocalypse* (with Rudolph Valentino, Alice Terry, Wallace Beery), 1921; *Blood and Sand* (with Rudolph Valentino, Lila Lee), 1922; *Enemies of Women* (with Lionel Barrymore, Alma Rubens), 1923; *Mare Nostrum* (with Alice Terry, Antonio Moreno), 1926; *The Torrent*—based on *Entre naranjos*— (with Greta Garbo, Ricardo Cortez), 1926; *The Temptress*—based on *La tierra de todos*—(with Greta Garbo, Antonio Moreno), 1926; *Blood and Sand* (with Tyrone Power, Linda Darnell, Rita Hayworth), 1941; *La barraca* (made in Mexico with Domingo Soler, Anita Blanch), 1944; *Mare Nostrum* (made in Mexico with María Félix, Fernando Rey, Nerio Bernardi), 1948; *Cañas y barro* (made in Italy and Spain with Anna Amendola, Virgilio Teixeira), 1954; and *The Four Horsemen of the Apocalypse* (with Glenn Ford, Ingrid Thulin, Charles Boyer), 1962.

6. José Padín, "Vicente Blasco Ibáñez," lecture at New York Public Library, 1928.

7. "Pigmalión," *Blasco Ibáñez, novelista* (Valencia, 1963), p. 84.

8. Gascó, p. 119.

9. José A. Balseiro, *Vicente Blasco Ibáñez, hombre de acción y de letras* (San Juan, Puerto Rico, 1935), p. 59.

Chapter Three

1. Even hostile critics admit that the Valencian group is a strong contribution. Nicolás González Ruíz, whose main basis for attack is that "Blasco is a declamatory and terrible anticlerical"—(*En este hora* [Madrid, 1925], p. 172)—concludes that the Valencian novels have "sobriety; they are intense, and the various types of people of Valencia are depicted with unquestionable skill." The citizens of the province were early aware of the honor done them. "Teodoro Llorente, unequivocally Catholic, monarchist, and conservative, but also unequiv-

ocally a journalist, poet, and man of letters, saluted with gladness the birth of this great Valencian novelist, for whom he predicted international fame. This is a glory which goes much beyond the merely literary, a glory which has nothing to do with the cenacle or the litterateurs, such as one recognizes, for example, in Madrid. It is a glory for all the people; better to say, broadly regional, which few Spaniards, since Cervantes and Lope, have received from their fellow citizens"— Martín Domínguez Barberá, *El tradicionalismo de un republicano* (Seville, 1961), p. 61.

2. Volume and page numbers in parentheses throughout all chapters are from V. Blasco Ibáñez, *Obras completas (Complete Works),* 3 vols. (Madrid, 1964).

3. Camille Pitollet, one of Blasco's early biographers, issued an anthology in chronological order of the Valencian author's descriptive passages entitled *Blasco Ibáñez, paisajista* (Paris, 1924).

4. "Passion—for a woman, for a sect, for the water of the river, for anything else—arouses the blood toward gallantry or toward betrayal; thus said Blasco, who knew how to draw from it such marked advantage. . . . Even a century ago, Señor Madoz lamented in his *Dictionary*: 'One will see with profound loathing that in the province of Valencia are to be found not only the inclination toward crimes of blood, but the fury with which these are committed' "—Joan Fuster, *El país valenciano* (Barcelona, 1964), p. 50.

5. *Rice and a Carriage* and the other Valencian novels provide much material for an excellent study, *El costumbrismo regional en la obra de Blasco Ibáñez* (Valencia, 1958), by Eduardo Betoret-París, a doctoral thesis at the University of Rochester. As the author of *Rice and a Carriage* says (p. 28): "The picture of the merchants, small *rentier* class, bourgeoisie, and, in general, the Valencian mesocracy is given in *Arroz y tartana,* through the pages of which parade many persons whom he knew in his childhood or whom his father or his father's friends talked about, unaware, surely, of the destiny or influence that these stories would have."

6. Andrés González Blanco, *Historia de la novela en España desde el romanticismo a nuestros días* (Madrid, 1909), p. 1019.

7. Although probably neither influenced the other, an odd similarity exists, in life and literature, between Blasco and Arnold Bennett, English author born in the same year. Both came from provincial towns, and their most secure fame rests on the half-dozen volumes of detailed regional realism—novels and short stories—that they wrote, drawing upon early experience. Both went as young men to the capital and became working journalists, essayists on literature, and voluminous producers of popular works on subjects ranging from travel to psychology. Both rose from the shopkeeping class to best-selling moneymakers and became possessors of châteaux in France, mingling

with cosmopolites without quite feeling at ease. Both revealed a power of making ordinary topics of sparkling interest to the reader, and likewise a vigorous appetite for living as well as writing. *The Old Wives' Tale* appeared in 1908, fourteen years after *Rice and a Carriage* (which had not yet been translated into English or French), and it is unlikely that Bennett ever read this novel by Blasco; but a comparison of the two books might reveal coincidences resulting from environmental influence and the spirit of the times. Both, for instance, deal with families of dry goods merchants who aspire to rise in the world.

8. González Blanco, p. 544.

9. *The Literature of the Spanish People*, 2nd ed. (Cambridge, England, 1953), p. 413.

10. The description of the Tribunal at the opening of Chapter 4 is an excellent example of Blasco's use of local color. This court, each official representing one of seven irrigation districts, has met at noon every Thursday for five hundred years, on the cathedral steps at the Puerta de los Apóstoles, guarded by images of the twelve apostles "so disfigured, so battered, that Jesus himself would not have recognized them" (I, 502). No records are kept. The visitor to Valencia today can attend this ancient ceremony and observe the patriarchal way in which rights are adjudicated by black-robed fellow farmers, and accepted as a Bedouin accepts the decree of his cadi at the tent door. As one writer has said: "Its proverbial justice, on the other hand, did not always prevent, in times of drought, and even in less menacing times, disputes between neighbors leading to treacherous gunshots: now the quarrels over water have lost their virulence, but the stories of Don Vicente Blasco were not pure inventions" (Fuster, p. 18).

11. The French translation of the book was entitled *Terres maudites*.

12. Brenan, p. 413.

Chapter Four

1. Zamacois, *Mis contemporáneos* (Madrid, 1910, 1928). An essay on *Entre naranjos* by Joaquín de Entrambasaguas, professor at the University of Madrid, precedes a reprint of the volume in *Las mejores novelas contemporáneas* (Barcelona, 1966), pp. 63–73.

2. *El tradicionalismo de un republicano* (Seville, 1961–1962), I, 67.

3. Domínguez Barberá, *loc. cit.*, I, 102. Blasco wrote to Julio Cejador in 1918: "*Sónnica* is, of all my novels, the least read in Spain, to judge by the number of printings. In Germany and in the United States, after translation, it enjoyed an enormous success, with many editions" (I, 18).

4. Quoted from dust wrapper of Editorial Planeta edition (Barcelona, 1958).

5. *Vicente Blasco Ibáñez e il suo capolavoro "Cañas y barro"* (Florence, 1922), III, 22.

6. This reclamation has continued. As a result of filling, the lake itself has shrunken from five thousand hectares in 1893 to a fourth of that area.

7. Andrés González Blanco, *Historia de la novela en España desde el romanticismo a nuestros días* (Madrid, 1909), p. 746.

8. *Mis contemporáneos,* p. 46.

9. James O. Swain, "The Albufera Thirty Years After: Memories of *Cañas y barro,*" *Hispania,* XVIII (Feb., 1935), 34.

10. *The Literature of the Spanish People,* 2nd ed. (Cambridge, England, 1953). p. 414.

Chapter 5

1. José A. Balseiro, *Vicente Blasco Ibáñez, hombre de acción y de letras* (San Juan, Puerto Rico, 1935), p. 38.

2. Elliott M. Grant comments on Zola's famous title in *Zola's "Germinal," A Critical and Historical Study* (Leicester, England, 1962), p. 12; see also notes pp. 36−37, 142: "It was the seventh month of the Revolutionary calendar, and one naturally thinks also of the events of the 12th of Germinal, in the third year of the Republic, when rioters invaded the Convention demanding 'bread and the Constitution of 1793.' But Zola was thinking less of that particular day than of the period of the year (March−April). . . . At first, it seemed to him 'too mystical, too symbolic.' But it represented what he was looking for: 'a revolutionary April, a flight of a decrepit, sick society into the springtime.' 'If the title is obscure to some readers,' he adds, 'it has become for me a flash of sunshine illuminating the whole work.' "

3. Actually, in the play that appeared in 1890, Death, the intruder, is not one of the dramatis personae. Her presence, however, is sensed by the others, and is foreshadowed by the entrance of illness. "Once that illness has entered a house, one might say that there is a stranger in the family"−Maurice Maeterlinck, *Théâtre,* I, 15th ed. (Brussels, 1908), 203.

4. Eduardo Betoret-París has assessed the use of dialect in *The Wine Cellar* and *Blood and Sand,* and finds the use of dialogue and dialectal forms greater in these than in novels with other settings (*El costumbrismo regional en la obra de Blasco Ibáñez* [Valencia, 1956], pp. 285−86, 313).

5. The force of the word *horda,* akin to the English "horde," as used in this novel seems to be somewhat dissipated by equating the word with "mob" or "rabble," as sometimes is done. In Chapter 1 the produce carts and their drivers are compared to "a prehistoric horde fleeing with hunger behind them and the desire for life, as a guide, ahead" (I, 1366). Again, in Chapter 12, Blasco uses the word *horda*

when speaking of Madrid, the city that could not see the hungry multitude scattered at its feet—"the horde which fed on its offal and filth, the girdle of living dung, of painful putrid matter." He adds that sometime or other "the horde would cease to remain motionless" (I, 1515). Maltrana expresses the wish that slaves of poverty, like himself, instead of remaining cowardly and offering themselves for the service of the mighty, could remain with their own people, placing in their hands what they had learned, striving to organize the horde into regiments, fusing its wild individuality of action into a common will.

Chapter Six

1. *Woman Triumphant,* tr. Hayward Keniston (New York, 1920).

2. Arthur Hamilton, in *A Study of Spanish Manners, 1750–1800 from the Plays of Ramón de la Cruz,* Univ. of Illinois Studies in Lang. and Lit., XI, No. 3, gives a good account (41–55) of the *majo* and his feminine counterpart, the *maja.* It makes clear that the *maja* took pride in being well dressed on gala occasions, and that she might be unmarried or married. All girl sellers of chestnuts, oranges, and limes, as well as most market women, many servants, and frequently the wives of honest artisans were *majas.*

3. Emilio Gascó Contell, *Genio y figura de Vicente Blasco Ibáñez* (Madrid, 1957), p. 95.

4. Page references for this novel, which is omitted from the *Collected Works,* refer to the posthumous edition (Barcelona, 1953).

5. In his youth Blasco had collaborated with Fernández y González on a novel, *El mocito de la fuentecilla,* about *toreros* and their sweethearts, which was termed by Eduardo Zamacois "a graceful sketch of customs, picturesque and glowing as a Goya painting"—*Mis contemporáneos,* I (Madrid, 1910), 5.

6. Quoted in Joaquín Casalduero, *Vida y obra de Galdós,* 2nd. ed. (Madrid, 1951), p. 32.

7. "Doctor Pardales" [pseudonym]. *Acontecimiento literario: ¿Es una imitación de "Niño bonito" y "El espada"? . . .* (Seville, 1908).

8. Gallardo's patronymic in Spanish is quite fitting; it means "elegant, magnanimous, gallant."

9. *Madó* is a form of address given in Mallorca to married women, or widows, of the low or middle class.

10. A term used in the Balearic Islands to designate the descendants of converted Jews.

11. *Papisa* means a woman pope, and is usually found in Spanish only with reference to the legendary character known in English as Pope Joan.

12. *Atlòta* means "girl" in Catalán. As Blasco uses it, the word seems to imply a lower social status, something like "peasant girl."

13. Olav K. Lundeberg in "The Sand-Chopin Episode in *Los muertos mandan*," *Hispania*, XV (1932), 135–40.

Chapter Seven

1. Blasco's remarks continue: "I had changed completely during the long fallow period. I wrote in another manner; my mentality was different; I saw life in more sure and vigorous terms. *The Argonauts* is a prologue. My intention was (and still is) to write a series of novels about the peoples of America who speak and think in Spanish. Spain lies not merely in Europe. Our province is nothing more than a peninsula of a spiritual and verbal Spain, which has twenty nations as departments, a great republic stretched over half the planet, bordering all the seas, beneath all the skies and latitudes, and whose ideal and unshakable president is Miguel de Cervantes. After *The Argonauts* I was going to write *The City of Hope* (Buenos Aires), *The Land of Everyone* (the countryside), and *The Murmurs of the Forest* (the lands still virgin). Then, two or three novels with a Chilean setting; another about Peru, *Gold and Death;* and thus I thought to keep on creating a group of novels with characters who would go to every Spanish-American region; something like the characters in *La comédie humaine* of Balzac. *The Argonauts* is no more than the prologue." Letter to Julio Cejador y Frauca, 1918 (I, 19). In a 1923 introduction to *The Argonauts* (II, 489–91) Blasco gives further information on the genesis of this novel.

2. This extract from an American review of *The Four Horsemen*, which went through about two hundred printings in the United States, is by no means unusual in its praise: "the greatest novel the war has produced.... It is primarily a great story, related with the art of a practiced novelist among whose virtues are sympathy and irony, delicacy and taste, honesty, conviction, and vision. Secondarily, it is a noteworthy history of the tragic days of France before the first Battle of the Marne"—Burton Rascoe in the Chicago *Tribune*, Oct. 19, 1918.

3. "The first proofs of *Mare Nostrum* were being printed when Blasco learned through the defense lawyer of the spy the details of the odyssey and death of Mata Hari. Then it was that he revised the ending of the work, and we may say that he took from reality the scene of the shooting, fusing it with his novelist's imaginings. With regard to the rest of the novel, the figure of Mata Hari not only did not influence Blasco Ibáñez in the creation of his Freya, but the novelist did not even know of her existence until months after having written and finished *Mare Nostrum*."—Emilio Gascó Contell, *Genio y figura de Vicente Blasco Ibáñez* (Madrid, 1957), pp. 178–79.

4. Unfavorable remarks about *Mare Nostrum* were offset by such enthusiasm as shown by the following tribute by a writer aroused by the coolness of such fellow authors as Pío Baroja and Ramón del

Valle-Inclán: "*Mare Nostrum* is the masterpiece of Blasco Ibáñez and the most beautiful, most intense, most filled with light and color, most implicative, most passionate, most profound, and most modern—O beloved vanguardists!—novel written in the twentieth century. It is magnificent, epic, and in robust imagination and in rich incident I compare this work of genius of Blasco Ibáñez to the *Odyssey*."—José Mas y Laglera, *Blasco Ibáñez y la jauría* (Madrid, 1928), pp. 80—81.

5. For other references to the *Gualicho* see III, 105 and 136, where—at the flight of Elena from the settlement—people say: "Let her leave. It is the *Gualicho* leaving us, after having upset everything. . . . Would that the demon would never return! If only she had left before!"

6. "Know that on the right hand of the Indies there is an island called California," runs a passage in *Las sergas de Esplandián,* "very close to the side of the Terrestrial Paradise; and it was peopled by black women, without any man among them, for they lived in the fashion of Amazons. Their island was the strongest in all the world, with its steep cliffs and rocky shores. Their arms were all of gold, and so was the harness of the wild beasts which they tamed to ride; for in the whole island there was no metal but gold." The gold rush to California, of course, did not take place until three centuries after the collapse of the Cortés colony.

Chapter Eight

1. Paul Winkler, "Last Words with Ibáñez," *Living Age,* 334 (1928), 399—402.

2. The term Gentleman-Mountain is used intentionally by Blasco to distinguish Edwin from earlier giant visitors, Gulliver being the first of a series. Cf. Jonathan Swift, *Gulliver's Travels,* ed. Ernest Bernbaum (New York: Harcourt, Brace, 1920), p. 28, for the explanation that the Great Man-Mountain was the interpretation of the Lilliputian words *Quinbus Flestrin.*

3. Swift, *ibid.,* p. 13: "in our passage from thence to the East-Indies, we were driven by a violent storm to the north-west of Van Diemen's Land." A note suggests that by Van Diemen's Land "perhaps Australia is meant."

4. *Saturday Review of Literature,* March 26, 1927, p. 678.

5. José María Salaverría, "Vicente Blasco Ibáñez," in *Enciclopedia universal ilustrada,* Series II, Appendix (Madrid, 1931), 293.

6. *Ibid.,* pp. 293—94.

7. The author states that Ojeda regarded this image as the best of his weapons; see also III, 1429, 1483.

8. See also III, 1429, where, after he had made love to the Indian queen Anacaona, Ojeda prays for forgiveness before the image of the Virgin Mary, his protector, and to his beloved Isabel Herboso, of whom

he had not thought for some time. For Isabel's becoming a nun and her subsequent death, see pp. 1436 and 1445.

Chapter Nine

1. Erasmo Buceta, in an article entitled "El origen de un cuento de Blasco Ibáñez," *Boletín de la Academia Española,* XX (1931), 93–96, gives as the source of this story an event that took place in Paris in January, 1908, related in *Le Temps* of January 4 in an article headed "Le suicide du comte Hasnic."

2. John B. Dalbor, "The Short Stories of Vicente Blasco Ibáñez" (Ann Arbor, Michigan: University Microfilms, 1961), pp. 285, 287–88.

Chapter Ten

1. "In Blasco Ibáñez throbs a social restlessness of anarchist lineage, quite in keeping with the decline of Romanticism—the nihilists of far-off Russia adapted to the air of London—and in the upshot, it is not at all unusual that the vestiges of a Romanticist should play their role within a Naturalist."—*Diccionario de literatura española,* 2nd ed. (Madrid, 1953), p. 95. And here is a sample of the sort of comment that could win a professorship in Madrid: "He [Blasco] passed his life like a fighter determined to triumph, and he succeeded, with astuteness using weapons of absolute efficacy in regions where vulgarity and nonsense prevailed. In spite of the working-class reformism of his early years, Blasco Ibáñez was a typical bourgeois of the left. He lacked, however, any spiritual or intellectual virtue. His philosophy of life (if he had one) is slippery. The spirit of Vicente Blasco Ibáñez is of an enormous vulgarity. His extraordinary vitality—his only authentic virtue—rejected all norms, from neckties to religious faith. The later years of his life reveal him as one whose sole purpose is to become wealthy. Few popular writers succeeded as did Blasco Ibáñez in reaching greater heights of contempt among his prominent contemporaries. It continues to be curious and paradoxical that, engaged in publishing enterprises, he was the first Spanish editor of Nietzsche. . . . His prose, like his life, is violent and vulgar. His sensibility picks up only the impetuous, the ordinary: he smells of sweat and sex, with savory fumes of *paella valenciana.*"—Gonzalo Torrente Ballester, *Panorama de la literatura española contemporánea,* 2nd ed. (Madrid, 1961), I, 129–30.

2. Varied opinions were expressed, for example, concerning Blasco's book *Mexican Militarism* (1921). Ramón Rosas y Reyes wrote a volume of four hundred pages to refute Blasco's charges. Yet a Spaniard, Luis de Oteyza, concluded: "The only book in Spanish that reflects with exactitude and fidelity the harvest of the Mexican Revolution is

Mexican Militarism by Blasco Ibáñez" (see José A. Balseiro, *Cuatro individualistas de España* [Chapel Hill, N.C., 1949], p. 72, n. 53).

3. Martín Domínguez Barberá, *El tradicionalismo de un republicano* (Sevilla, 1961), I, 10—11.

4. *Las mejores novelas contemporáneas* (Barcelona, 1966), II, 52—53.

5. *In Memoriam: Libro-homenaje al inmortal novelista V. Blasco Ibáñez* (Valencia, 1929).

6. Introduction to *The Shadow of the Cathedral* (New York, 1919).

7. *The Soul of Spain* (London, 1924), p. 413.

8. "Blasco Ibáñez, 1867—1928," *Nineteenth Century,* CIII (Jan.— June, 1928), 559.

9. *The Literature of the Spanish People,* 2nd ed. (Cambridge, England, 1953), pp. 411—14.

10. Balseiro, José A., *Cuatro individualistas de España* (Chapel Hill, N.C., 1949), p. 62.

11. From Julio Cejador y Frauca, *Historia de la lengua y literatura castellana,* IX (Madrid, 1918).

12. Quoted in Balseiro, p. 71.

13. *Ibid.* Barja gives a similarly clear description of the typical structure: "His novel is of that type that . . . begins *in medias res,* with an advanced chapter of the story, although not an essential part of the principal action, in which are presented to us one or more of the chief characters, and an impression of the atmosphere in which the action will develop is formed. Then, in the next chapter, begins the real action . . . and thus the development continues, in broad sketches, in long—sometimes heavy—chapters. Many of these chapters could easily be separated and would live by themselves, as finished pictures, as complete scenes. But although the action does not answer to a principle of strict unity, and the movement is rather external than internal, there is an essential linking and unity of setting, and the entire novel is finally fused into an artistic whole, into an organic unity."—César Barja, *Libros y autores modernos,* 2nd ed. (New York: Las Américas), 1964, p. 401.

14. Camilo Pitollet, *Blasco Ibáñez* (Valencia, 1921), pp. 207—8.

15. Miguel Angel Escalante, "Notas sobre el estilo de Vicente Blasco Ibáñez," *Cultura,* II (1950), 69. This brief essay is one of the few analytic studies of Blasco's style.

16. Joaquín de Entrambasaguas (ed.), *Las mejores novelas contemporáneas* (Barcelona, 1966), II, 51—52.

17. *Historia de la literatura española* (New York, 1948), II, 148.

18. *Ibid.,* p. 152.

19. Balseiro, p. 13.

20. *Enciclopedia universal ilustrada* (Madrid: Espasa-Calpe, 1920), VIII, 1119.

21. *Cassell's Encyclopedia of World Literature* (New York, 1954), II, 1710.

22. Joaquín Casalduero, *Vida y obra de Galdós,* 2nd ed. (Madrid, 1961), p. 28.

23. "Only one character—or we may say one type—is there in Blasco's novels that is fully achieved, presented with dimensions and strength, felt and understood. It corresponds entirely to the philosophy, psychology, and even to the physiology of Blasco Ibáñez himself."—Barja, *op. cit.,* p. 396.

24. Quoted in Ayuntamiento de Valencia, Publicaciones del Archivo Municipal, *Vicente Blasco Ibáñez* (Valencia, 1933), p. 60. César Barja also lauds Blasco's endeavor to present the historical volumes about Spain and the New World: "It was a happy idea on the part of the author to write these novels, and it is to be regretted that he was not able to complete the series. With it he would have performed a fine service to his country, helping in a work of reevaluation which, especially with regard to the conquest and behavior of Spain in America, is already in progress, but to which a novelist like Blasco Ibáñez would have made a great contribution by popularizing. It was, doubtless, the noblest tribute which the author could think of dedicating to his country, and an honorable and worthy end to a work which he had begun with Spain and with criticisms of Spanish life."—Barja, *op. cit.,* pp. 413–14.

Selected Bibliography

Blasco Ibáñez published more than sixty books, but many of them were on historical or political subjects, or were topical works or early romances he did not wish to have remembered.

These early romances, written under the influence of Manuel Fernández y González, were published around 1888 to 1892; they were probably turned out to earn a living and to obtain money on which to get married. They were later rejected by Blasco as being unworthy of preservation, and he speaks of *Arroz y tartana* (1894) as his "first novel." The romances include such titles as *El conde Garci-Fernández, Por la patria (Romeu el guerrillero), El adiós de Schubert, El conde de Balsega, El padre Claudio, El señor Avellaneda, El capitán Alvárez* (2 vols.), *La señora de Quirós, Ricardito Balsega, Marujita Quirós, Juventud a la sombra de la vejes, En París, El casamiento de María, El final de Norma,* and *Fantasías, leyendas y tradiciones* (short stories). Two two-volume works appeared in 1892. *La araña negra (The Black Spider),* written in Paris and inspired by Eugene Sue's *The Wandering Jew,* deals with Jesuit cunning and deception. *¡Viva la república!* tells the adventures of a young Spaniard named Guzmán, refugee from the Inquisition in Seville, who joins the Jacobins in the French Revolution and dies a martyr to liberty, equality, and fraternity. Around 1925 a Madrid firm, Editorial Cosmópolis, despite Blasco's objections, capitalized on his name and fame by reprinting some of the early romances in paperback format.

Blasco was the most widely translated of all modern Spanish writers and probably, along with H. G. Wells, the most internationally popular of his generation. Hence only first Spanish and first English editions of his books will be listed below. A good list of other translations is given by Gascó Contell, pp. 219–25 (see *Secondary Sources* below).

No attempt is here made to include any of the hundreds of periodical articles by Blasco Ibáñez. As he wrote in the preface to his *Militarismo mexicano* (II, 1446): "I have collected in volumes my stories (not all of them) and some essays on literature (very few). I have never considered worthy of collecting in editions my writings on politics, sociology, history, etc. I was a journalist for fifteen years, and I wrote an article or two every day."

All first editions of Blasco's novels were printed under his supervision by Editorial Prometeo (Sempere, Llorca y Cía.) of Valencia, a publishing house destroyed in the Civil War of 1936–1939, and texts of other editions may not be definitive. The collected works in three volumes listed below, published by Aguilar in Madrid, comprise thirty-six works but exclude several listed under "Books" below. Twenty-two volumes of fiction appear in the series issued by Editorial Planeta, Barcelona, and most of Blasco's popular works are published in the Colección Austral, Buenos Aires. Blasco's chief publisher in English is E. P. Dutton, New York and London; all translations below were issued by Dutton unless otherwise noted. For literal translations of all important titles, see the Chronology.

PRIMARY SOURCES

1. *Collections.*

Obras completas (Complete Works), 11 vols. Valencia: Prometeo, 1925. Contains *La barraca, Flor de mayo, La horda, El intruso, Los Argonautas, En el país del arte, Los cuatro jinetes del apocalipsis, Los muertos mandan, Los enemigos de la mujer,* and *Sónnica la cortesana.*

Obras completas, with anonymous bibliographic note, 3 vols. Madrid: Aguilar, 1946. Contains thirty-six works.

The Last Lion and Other Tales. Boston: Four Seas, 1919. Contains "The Last Lion," "The Toad," "Compassion," "The Windfall," "Luxury," and "Rabies." (Originally published in Spanish in *Luna Benamor,* 1909.)

The Old Woman of the Movies, New York, 1925. Various translators. Contains, in addition to the title story, "The Hero," "The Widow's Loan," "A Shot in the Night," "Sunset," "The Four Sons of Eve," "The Caburé Feather," "The Serenade," "The General's Automobile," "Martínez' Insurrection," "A Life Sentence," "A Serbian Night," "The Monster," "The Sleeping Car Porter," and "The Mad Virgins." (Originally most of these were published in Spanish in *El préstamo de la difunta,* 1921.)

2. *Books: Fiction.*

(As stated, only the dates of first editions are given, in chronological order—first the Spanish date, then the English.)

Arroz y tartana, 1895. *The Three Roses,* tr. S. E. Grummon, 1932.
Cuentos valencianos, 1896.

Flor de mayo, 1896. *The Mayflower*, tr. Arthur Livingston, New York, 1921.

La barraca, 1898. *The Cabin*, tr. Francis Haffkine-Snow and Beatrice M. Mekota (New York: Boni & Liveright, 1919).

Entre naranjos, 1900. *The Torrent*, tr. Isaac Goldberg and Arthur Livingston, New York, 1921.

La condenada, 1900.

Sónnica la cortesana, 1901. *Sonnica the Courtesan*, tr. Frances Douglas (New York: Duffield, 1912).

Cañas y barro, 1902. *Reeds and Mud*, tr. Isaac Goldberg, New York, 1928.

La catedral, 1903. *The Shadow of the Cathedral*, tr. Mrs. W. A. Gillespie, New York, 1919.

El intruso, 1904. *The Intruder*, tr. Mrs. W. A. Gillespie, New York, 1928.

La voluntad de vivir, 1904 (all but one copy destroyed by the author; this novel was reprinted in 1953 by Editorial Planeta, Barcelona).

La bodega, 1905. *The Fruit of the Vine*, tr. Isaac Goldberg, New York, 1919.

La horda, 1905. *The Mob*, tr. M. J. Llorente, New York, 1929.

La maja desnuda, 1906. *Woman Triumphant*, tr. Hayward Keniston, New York, 1920.

Sangre y arena, 1908. *The Blood of the Arena*, tr. Frances Douglas (Chicago: A. C. McClurg, 1911). *Blood and Sand*, tr. Mrs. W. A. Gillespie, New York, 1919.

Los muertos mandan, 1909. *The Dead Command*, tr. Frances Douglas (New York: Duffield, 1919).

Luna Benamor, 1909. *Luna Benamor*, tr. Isaac Goldberg (Boston: J. L. Luce, 1919).

Los Argonautas, 1914.

Los cuatro jinetes del Apocalipsis, 1916. *The Four Horsemen of the Apocalypse*, tr. Charlotte Brewster Jordan, New York, 1918.

Mare Nostrum, 1918. *Our Sea*, tr. Charlotte Brewster Jordan, New York, 1919.

Los enemigos de la mujer, 1919. *The Enemies of Women*, tr. I. Brown, 1920.

El préstamo de la difunta, 1920.

La tierra de todos, 1921. *The Temptress*, tr. Leo Ongley, New York, 1923.

El paraíso de las mujeres, 1922.

La reina Calafia, 1923. *Queen Calafia*, New York, 1924. No translator cited.

Novelas de la costa azul, 1924.

El papa del mar, 1925. *The Pope of the Sea*, tr. Arthur Livingston, New York, 1927.

A los pies de Venus, 1926. *The Borgias; or At the Feet of Venus,* tr. Arthur Livingston, New York, 1930.

Novelas de amor y de muerte, 1927.

En busca del Gran Kan, 1929. *Unknown Lands (The Story of Columbus),* tr. Arthur Livingston, New York, 1929.

El Caballero de la Virgen, 1929. *Knight of the Virgin,* tr. Arthur Livingston, New York, 1930.

El fantasma de las alas de oro, 1930. The Phantom with Wings of Gold, tr. Arthur Livingston, New York, 1931.

3. *Books: Selected Miscellaneous Works.*

Historia de la revolución española, 1808–1874, 3 vol. Barcelona: la Enciclopedia Democrática, 1892; Madrid: Cosmopólis, 1930.

París, impresiones de un emigrado. Valencia: Prometeo, 1893.

El juez (play). Valencia: Ripollés, 1894.

En el país del arte. Valencia: Prometeo, 1896. *In the Land of Art,* tr. Frances Douglas, New York: Dutton, 1923.

Novísima geografía universal, por Onesime Reclús y J. J. E. Reclús, tr. from French, with preface, by V. Blasco Ibáñez, 6 vols. Madrid: La Novela Ilustrada, 1906–1907.

Oriente. Valencia: Prometeo, 1907.

Novísima historia universal, dirigida a partir del siglo IV, por Ernesto Lavisse y Alfredo Rambaud, tr. from French by V. Blasco Ibáñez, 15 vols. Madrid: A. Marzo; Valencia: Prometeo, 1908–1930.

Argentina y sus grandezas. Madrid: Editorial Española Americana, 1910.

El libro de los mil y una noches por J. C. Mardrus, tr. from French by V. Blasco Ibáñez, 23 vols. Valencia: Prometeo, 1915.

Historia de la guerra europea de 1914, 13 vols. Valencia: Prometeo, 1914–1919.

El militarismo mejicano. Valencia: Prometeo, 1920. *Mexico in Revolution,* tr. José Padín and Arthur Livingston, New York: Dutton, 1920.

Estudios literarios. Valencia: Prometeo, 1933.

Una nación secuestrada: Alfonso XIII desenmascarado. Paris: J. Durá, 1924. *Alfonso XIII Unmasked: The Military Terror of Spain,* tr. Arthur Livingston and José Padín. New York: Dutton, 1924.

Lo que será la república española: al país y al ejército. Valencia: La Gutenberg, 1925.

La vuelta al mundo de un novelista, 3 vols. Valencia: Prometeo, 1924–1925. *A Novelist's Tour of the World,* tr. Leo Ongley and Arthur Livingston. New York: Dutton, 1926.

Discursos literarios. Valencia: Prometeo, 1966.

SECONDARY SOURCES

A large number of references, good and mediocre, could be cited. Almost all, however, appear solely in languages other than English, and few are readily accessible to the nonspecialists. Items considered worthy of annotation are given below. Lengthy but unannotated bibliographies appear in the *Obras completas* (I, 21); in Balseiro, pp. 74–76; in Betoret-París, pp. 335–42; in Dalbor, pp. 292–303; in Entrambasaguas, pp. 75–81; in Gascó Contell, pp. 23–24; and in León Roca, pp. 620–60. A number of other sources used in this book are cited earlier in the Notes and References.

AYUNTAMIENTO DE VALENCIA. Publicaciones del Archivo Municipal. *Vicente Blasco Ibáñez*. Valencia: La Gutenberg, 1933. A pamphlet issued by the Municipal Archives and Historical Museum of the City of Valencia to celebrate the reburial of Blasco in his native city. It contains a chronology, several fragments of Blasco's writing in the Valencian dialect, and eight pages of laudatory comments by various contributors.

BALSEIRO, JOSE A. *Cuatro individualistas de España*. Chapel Hill, N.C.: University of North Carolina Press, 1949, pp. 3–76. A highly useful brief biography, with critical comments, by a poet and novelist born in Puerto Rico, who served on the faculties of Duke University and the University of Miami.

BARJA, CESAR. *Libros y autores modernos*. 2nd ed. New York: Las Américas, 1964. The final chapter of this balanced critical study of Spain's leading writers of the eighteenth and nineteenth centuries is devoted to Blasco Ibáñez. Barja stresses Blasco's success in depicting the hero of action—with whom the novelist had much in common—as well as the vigor and masculinity of his temperament and art. In particular, Barja believes Blasco may well be the best Spanish author in the field of the regional novel.

BETORET-PARIS, EDUARDO. *El costumbrismo regional en la obra de Blasco Ibáñez*. Valencia: Fomento de Cultura Ediciones, 1958. This thesis for an American doctorate analyzes the regionalist aspects of Blasco's art. The author concludes that "Blasco, an artist by intuition and by temperament, was unable to conceive a character without surrounding him with an adequate environment in all its aspects, whether geographic, racial, social, ideological, economic, genre, or linguistic—and above all, those relating to the region and the theme undertaken in his works."

BRENAN, GERALD. *The Literature of the Spanish People*, 2nd ed. Cambridge, England: Cambridge University Press, 1953. Contains *passim* some highly luadatory remarks on Blasco's achievement.

CEJADOR y FRAUCA, JULIO. *Historia de la lengua y literatura castellana*. 14 vols. Madrid: *Revista de Archivos, Bibliotecas y*

Museos, 1915–1922, IX (1918), 467–80. A brief but quite balanced account. The invaluable letter from Blasco to Cejador, which appears on pp. 471–80, is reprinted in *Obras completas,* I, 14–20.

DALBOR, JOHN BRONISLAW. *The Short Stories of Vicente Blasco Ibáñez.* Ann Arbor, Mich.: University Microfilms, 1961. An excellent dissertation (University of Michigan, 1961) dealing with the short story in general, the Spanish *cuento,* Blasco's literary theories, and examination of his short stories.

DOMINGUEZ BARBERA, MARTIN. *El tradicionalismo de un republicano.* 3 vols. Seville: Montejura, 1962. A valuable recent study by a Valencian compatriot of Blasco, in which biography and criticism are enhanced by historical excursions. The main argument of the volume is that, paradoxically, Blasco, apparently a radical and iconoclast, was rooted in the rich Mediterranean—specifically Valencian—tradition. This background enabled him to adventure beyond provincial limitations and to explore America and the rest of Europe with a sound intellectual and moral inheritance. The author assumes that the reader is familiar with the content of Blasco's books.

ENTRAMBASAGUAS, JOAQUIN de. *Las mejores novelas contemporáneas,* II. Barcelona: Planeta, 1966, pp. 4–81. This introduction to a reprint of *Entre naranjos* includes as well a general essay on Blasco and a bibliography. For biography the essay depends heavily on Gascó Contell, "nearly the sole biographer worthy of esteem."

ESCALANTE, MIGUEL ANGEL. "Notas sobre el estilo de Vicente Blasco Ibáñez," *Cultura* (Buenos Aires), II (1950), 69. This brief essay is one of the few analytic studies of Blasco's style.

GASCO CONTELL, EMILIO. *Genio y figura de Blasco Ibáñez, agitador, aventurero y novelista.* Madrid: Afrodisio Aguado, 1957, 1967. This foremost biography of Blasco was written by a friend and fellow Valencian who as a young man worked for Blasco's publishing firm and who later encountered the author in Nice and Paris. It contains a number of useful appendixes and excellent illustrations.

GONZALEZ BLANCO, ANDRES. *Historia de la novela en España desde el romanticismo a nuestros días.* Madrid: Sáenz de Jubera, 1909. An early but useful source; the author associates Blasco with the decline of nineteenth-century Naturalism.

HOWELLS, WILLIAM DEAN. "The Fiction of Blasco Ibáñez," *Harpers,* CXXXI (1915), 957–60. An early appreciation by the foremost American critic of his time.

IN MEMORIAM: *Libro-homenaje al inmortal novelista V. Blasco Ibáñez.* Valencia: Prometeo, 1929. A memorial volume with a number of essays by various hands, as well as several pages of eulogies by writers of more or less importance.

LEON ROCA, J. L. *Vicente Blasco Ibáñez. Valencia: Prometeo, 1967.* Numerous clear illustrations add to the attractiveness of this recent, detailed study of the author's life. This is probably the most useful biography of Blasco in Spanish, replete with quotations from lesser-known newspapers and other periodicals.

MARTINEZ de la RIVA, RAMON. *Blasco Ibáñez, su vida, su obra, su muerte, sus mejores páginas.* Madrid: Mundo Latino, 1929. An anthology with some useful comment; the editor, in general, prefers the Valencian to the later novels.

MAS y LAGLERA, JOSE. *Blasco Ibáñez y la jauría.* Madrid: Renacimiento, 1928. A fervid defense issued shortly after Blasco's death by a friend who attacks the coolness of other Spaniards—the "pack of hounds"—towards the author's achievements. "Blasco has been," the author says, "and will continue to be, the only Spanish novelist who succeeded in attracting to his person the attention of the world."

NICHOLSON, HELEN S. "The Novel of Protest and the Spanish Republic." University of Arizona *Bulletin,* Humanities Bulletin No. 3 (Tucson, Ariz.: University of Arizona, July 1, 1939). Blasco's works of social protest are featured in this lecture, together with others by Pío Baroja, Ramón Pérez de Ayala, and Concha Espina, for their significance in foreshadowing Spain's Second Republic, established in 1931.

ORTEGA, JOAQUIN. "Vicente Blasco Ibáñez," *University of Wisconsin Studies,* XX (1924), 214–38 (Madison, Wisc.: University of Wisconsin). This study attempts an impartial evaluation of Blasco's artistry. The critic states that the novelist is "unique as a writer of lyrical descriptions in all literature. His novels render external reality seen through a powerfully subjective temperament. . . . Blasco is above all a painter, a great impressionist painter," like his fellow Valencian Joaquín Sorolla. The pity is that Blasco went beyond this aim, where his abilities were unrivalled, to give us "many later works in which psychology, philosophy, and pure intellect have a very relative value."

PEMAN, JOSE MARIA. "Blasco Ibáñez en América," *Mundo hispánico,* No. 228 (March, 1967), 10. A brief memoir of Blasco's reception as a lecturer in Argentina.

"PIGMALION" [JOSE MELIA]. *Blasco Ibáñez, novelista.* Valencia: Pastor, 1963. A rather rambling lecture delivered in London in 1958 contains some useful anecdotes as well as literary comments.

PITOLLET, CAMILO. *Vicente Blasco Ibáñez: sus novelas y la novela de su vida.* Tr. from the French by Tulio Moncada. Valencia:

Prometeo, 1921. A French admirer wrote this enthusiastic critique, which Professor Entrambasaguas terms "a panegyric verging on the ridiculous, written soon after Blasco's pro-French propaganda." Some statements and opinions cannot be supported by the facts. Disappointed by the reception of his book, Pitollet swung to the other extreme, and in his undated pamphlet *Gloses* (Lille/Paris) he attacked Blasco violently—among the mildest of his epithets is "insatiable pirate." See also Pitollet's explanation, "Como escribí el libro sobre Blasco Ibáñez," *Boletín de la Biblioteca Menéndez y Pelayo*, XXXIII (1957), 345—46.

REDING, CATHERINE. "Blasco Ibáñez and Zola," *Hispania*, VI (Dec., 1923), 365—71. The writer concludes that Zola's work supplied suggestions to Blasco, especially for the latter's earlier works, but Blasco did not use them in the same form. "Rather did he assimilate them, then express them, modified by his own personality, augmented by his individual concepts and experiences, and made thoroughly Spanish."

STARKIE, WALTER. "Blasco Ibáñez, 1867—1928." *Nineteenth Century*, CIII (Jan.—June, 1928), 542—59. An obituary essay containing measured critical comment, by an English author well acquainted with Spain.

SWAIN, JAMES O. "The Albufera Thirty Years After: Memories of *Cañas y barro*," *Hispania*, XVIII (Feb., 1935), 25—34. A pilgrimage to the marshland south of Valencia, scene of *Reeds and Mud*, arouses further appreciation of this early novel.

ZAMACOIS, EDUARDO. *Mis contemporáneos, I: Vicente Blasco Ibáñez*. Madrid: Sucesores de Hernando, 1910. An early but quite sound commentary containing biographical details.

Index

The Spanish system is herein used, by which the patronymic precedes the name of the maternal grandparent. For example, the works of V. Blasco Ibáñez appear under "Blasco." However, the names of some persons known to the English-speaking world, such as V. Núñez Balboa, are cross-indexed under the last name. Fictitious persons, places, or ships are not indexed. Actual streets, parks, buildings, churches, holidays, songs, publishers, publications, and other items that the reader would not readily recall are also omitted.

Achilles, 91
Adonis-Baldur, 87
Aeneid, 52
Africa, 22, 114
Aguilar de Alfambra, 18, 138
Alboraya, 54
Albufera, La, 42, 57, 64-67, 143
Alcaide, 140
Alcira, 57
Alexander VI, 107, 109
Alfonso XII, 22
Alfonso XIII, 29, 40, 120
Alfonso the Magnanimous, 24
Algiers, 43, 46, 48, 49
Also sprach Zarathustra, 79
Amadeus, King, 22
Amadís de Gaula, 101
Amazons, 39, 101, 111, 146
Amendola, A., 140
America, 39, 53, 96, 99, 106, 129, 136, 145
Americas, 8, 91
Andalusia, 69, 76, 80
Andes, 34, 41, 117
Andrea Chenier, 119
Anna Karenina, 64
Aphrodite, 61

Apocalypse, The, 95
Apollonius (of Rhodes), 91
Apuleius, 62
Arabs, 18, 138
Aragón, 7, 18, 123
Aranjuez, 30, 117
Argentina, 8, 17, 32-35, 91, 93, 94, 96, 99, 100, 117, 120, 121
Argonauts, 91, 93
Argüello, Concha, 101
Asia, 61
Athens, 119
Atlantic Ocean, 35, 39, 61, 136
Avignon, 39, 106, 107
Avila, 30
Australia, 105, 115, 146
"Azorín," 25, 134
Aztecs, 33

Bakunin, M. A., 71, 73
Balboa, *see* Núñez
Balearic Islands, 62, 80, 144
Balkans, 31, 119
Balseiro, J. A., 38, 124, 133, 134, 139, 140, 143, 148
Balzac, H. de, 21, 38, 43, 134, 145
Barca family, 62

159

Barcelona, 22, 32, 71
Barja, C., 148, 149
Baroja, P., 145
Barrymore, L., 97, 140
Bayonne, 53
Bedouin, 141
Beery, W., 94, 140
Beethoven, L. van, 27, 30, 70, 73, 95, 133
Begoña, 75
Benedict XIII, *see* Luna, Pedro de
Benlliure, brothers, 30, 43
Bennett, A., 48, 141, 142
Berkeley, Calif., 100
Berlin, 94
Bernardi, N., 97, 140
Bernbaum, E., 146
Berne, 31, 119
Betoret-París, E., 141, 143
Bible, 35, 95
Bilbao, 29, 69, 73, 75, 76
Blanch, A., 146
Blasco, J. C., 139
Blasco, Libertad, 139
Blasco, M., 139
Blasco, R., 138
Blasco, S., 139
Blasco del Cacho, María, 21, 40, 139
Blasco Ibáñez, V.: ancestry, 18, 20; birth, 18; biography, 19 ff.; marriages, 21, 33, 40; children, 22, 139; death, 41; also *passim*.

WRITINGS OF (see also Bibliography)
A los pies de Venus (*At the Feet of Venus*), 39, 104, 108, 109
"Adiós de Schubert, El" ("Schubert's Farewell"), 113
Aguila y la Serpiente, El (*The Eagle and the Serpent*), 38, 120
Alfonso XIII desenmascarado (*Alfonso XIII Unmasked*), 40, 120
"Amor y la muerte, El" ("Love and Death"), 117
Araña negra, La (*The Black Spider*), 75, 76, 84
Argentina y sus grandezas (*Argentina and Its Grandeurs*), 33, 120
Argonautas, Los (*The Argonauts*), 35, 38, 39, 78, 90-93, 101, 109, 145

Arroz y tartana (*Rice and a Carriage*), 18, 19, 41, 42, 44, 46-48, 51, 114, 131, 138, 141, 142
"Automóvil del general, El" ("The General's Automobile"), 78, 118
Barraca, La (*The Cabin*), 24, 27, 28, 41, 42, 44, 50, 52-54, 56. 114, 133, 140
"Beso, Un" ("A Kiss"), 118
Bodega, La (*The Wine Cellar*), 30, 69, 76, 81, 137
Caballero de la Virgen, El (*The Knight of the Virgin*), 39, 104, 110
"Caperuza, La" ("The Cape"), 114
Cañas y Barro (*Reeds and Mud*), 28, 38, 42, 59, 61, 64, 114, 140, 143
"Casa del Labrador, La" ("The Laborer's Cottage"), 117
Catedral, La (*The Cathedral*), 28, 30, 69-71, 73, 74, 76, 81, 82, 101, 134, 135
"Cencerrada, La" ("The Serenade"), 114
"Comediante Fonseca, El" ("Fonseca the Actor"), 118
"Compasión" ("Compassion"), 116
Condenada, La (*The Condemned Woman*), 26, 43, 114, 119
"Cosa de Hombres" ("Male Affairs"), 114
"Cuatro hijos de Eva, Los" ("The Four Sons of Eve"), 118
Cuatro jinetes del Apocalipsis, Los (*The Four Horsemen of the Apocalypse*), 7, 29, 35, 36, 90, 93-97, 105, 133, 136, 137, 140, 145
Cuentos valencianos (*Valencian Tales*), 42, 43, 113, 119
"Despertar del Buda, El" ("The Awakening of the Buddha"), 118
"Devorada, La" ("The Devouring Woman"), 119
"Dimoni" ("Demon"), 113
Discursos Literarios (*Literary Lectures*), 120, 121
"Empleado del coche-cama, El" ("The Sleeping Car Porter"), 118
En busca del Gran Kan (*In Search of the Great Khan*), 39, 104, 109, 110

En el país del arte (*In the Land of Art*), 26, 119

"En la costa azul" ("On the Côte d'Azur"), 118

Enemigos de la mujer, Los (*The Enemies of Women*), 35, 90, 97, 98, 100, 112, 140

Entre naranjos (*Among the Orange Trees*), 28, 37, 42, 43, 57, 59, 60, 82, 130, 140, 142

Estudios literarios (*Literary Studies*), 120, 134

"Familia del doctor Pedraza, La" ("Dr. Pedraza's Family"), 118

Fantasías, leyendas y tradiciones (*Fantasies, Legends, and Traditions*), 113

Fantasma de las alas de oro, El (*The Phantom with Wings of Gold*), 39, 41, 104, 112

"'Femater,' El" ("The Trash Collector"), 114

Flor de mayo (*The Mayflower*), 20, 41-43, 48-52, 64, 133, 139

"Golpe doble" ("A Shot in the Dark"), 114

"Hallazgo, Un" ("A Find"), 116

Historia de la guerra europea de 1914 (*History of the European War of 1914*), 35

Historia de la revolución española, 1808-1874 (*History of the Spanish Revolution, 1808-1874*), 21

"Hombre al agua" ("Man in the Water"), 114

Horda, La (*The Horde*), 30, 38, 69, 78-82, 91

Intruso, El (*The Intruder*), 28, 30, 69, 73-75, 80, 82

Juez, El (*The Judge*), 22

"Loca de la casa, La" ("The Madwoman of the House"), 118

"Lujo, El" ("Luxury"), 116

Luna Benamor, 80, 115, 116

"Madre tierra, La" ("Mother Earth"), 117

Mare Nostrum (*Our Sea*), 7, 20, 29, 35, 90, 97, 101, 137, 140, 145, 146

Militarismo mejicano, El (*Mexican Militarism*), 38, 120, 147, 148

"Monstruo, El" ("The Monster"), 117

Muertos mandan, Los (*The Dead Command*), 31, 80, 87-89, 115, 137, 145

"Noche de bodas" ("Wedding Night"), 114

"Noche servia" ("Serbian Night"), 118

Novelas de la costa azul (*Stories of the Côte d'Azur*), 118

Novelas de amor y de muerte (*Stories of Love and Death*), 118

Maja Desnuda, La (*The Naked Maja*), 78-82, 91, 137

Obras completas (*Collected Works*), 9, 122, 124, 138, 139

"Ogro, El" ("The Ogre"), 114

Oriente (*Orient*), 31, 119, 120

Papa del Mar, El (*The Pope of the Sea*), 39, 104, 106, 108, 109

Paraíso de mujeres, El (*The Paradise of Women*), 37, 104-6

"Parásito del tren, El" ("The Parasite of the Train"), 114

"Pared, La" ("The Wall"), 114

"Piedra de luna" ("Moonstone"), 119

"Plumas del caburé, Las" ("The Caburé Feathers"), 118

Préstamo de la difunta, El (*The Dead Woman's Loan*), 117, 119

"Primavera triste" ("Sad Spring"), 114

"Puesta del sol" ("Sunset"), 118

"Rabia, La" ("Rabies"), 116

Reina Calafia, La (*Queen Calafia*), 39, 90, 101, 104

"Réprobo, El" ("The Reprobate"), 119

"Rey Lear, impresor, El" ("King Lear, Printer"), 119

"Rosas y ruiseñores" ("Roses and Nightingales"), 117

Sangre y arena (*Blood and Sand*), 7, 31, 35, 37, 38, 80, 82, 84, 86, 137, 140

"Sapo, El" ("The Toad"), 116

"Secreto de la baronesa, El" ("The Secret of the Baroness"), 119

"Sol de los muertos, El" ("The Sunshine of the Dead"), 118

Sónnica la cortesana (*Sónnica the Courtesan*), 28, 42, 43, 60, 61, 130, 135, 142

"Sublevación de Martínez, La" ("The Insurrection of Martínez"), 118

Tierra de todos, La (*The Land of Everyone*), 37, 90, 99, 104, 140

"Torre de la Boatella, La" ("The Boatella Tower"), 19, 113

"Último leon, El" ("The Last Lion"), 116

"Vejez, La" ("Old Age"), 117

"Viejo del paseo de los ingleses, El" ("The Old Man of the Promenade des Anglais"), 118

"Vieja del 'cinema', La" ("The Old Woman of the Movies"), 118

"Vírgenes locas, Las" ("The Mad Virgins"), 118

Voluntad de vivir, La (*The Will to Live*), 9, 30. 80, 82

Vuelta al mundo de un novelista, La (*A Novelist's Tour of the World*), 39, 120

Blasco-Ibáñez Tortosa, V., 139

Blasco Teruel, G., 18, 138

Blasco y Moreno, R., 21

Blasquistas, 7, 25, 27

"Bombita," 86

Bonaparte, J., 22, 65

Borbón, J. de, 40

Bordeaux, 31

Borgia family, 39, 104, 108

Boyer, C., 94, 140

Brenan, G., 52, 56, 68, 124, 142

Buceta, E., 147

Budapest, 31, 119

Buenos Aires, 32, 91, 92, 94, 115, 118, 119

Buffon, Comte de, 130

Burjasot, 19, 46

Burma, 120

Cadiz, 61

Calatayud, 18, 138

Calcutta, 120

Calixtus III, 107

California, 39, 99, 101, 146

Californians, 101, 102

Callao, 51

Cannae, 64

Cánovas del Castillo, A., 21

Cantabrian coast, 118

Cap Milano (ship), 32

Cape Bagur, 43

Carlists, 22, 75

Carmen, 84

Carranza, V., 38, 120

Carthage, 60, 63

Carthaginians, 18, 63

Casalduero, J., 144, 149

Castellón de la Plana, 21, 25, 107

Castrovedo, R., 27

Catalans, 18

Cataluña, 18

Catedral, .4, 73

Catédrale, La, 73

Catholic Church, 19, 21, 31, 59, 69, 72, 74, 79, 134, 135

Cato, 63

Cejador y Frauca, J., 124-127, 130, 133, 142, 145, 148

Cervantes, M., 7, 17, 30, 32, 41, 121, 125, 128, 132-34, 141, 145

Cervantes (city), 34

Ceylon, 39, 120

Charles IV, 117

Chekhov, A., 119

Chile, 32, 33, 41, 117, 139, 145

China, 39, 109, 120

Chopin, F., 88, 89, 145

Christ, 67

Christians, 138

Cid, El, 91

Circe, 96

Civil Guard, 26, 77, 79, 114

Clemenceau, G., 31

Clement V., 107

Clement VI., 106

Collier, W., Jr., 97

Columbus, C., 39, 41, 91, 104, 106, 109, 110, 135

Comédie humaine, La, 43, 145

Comte, A., 134

Constance, 119

Constantinople, 31, 101, 119

Corrientes, 34

Cortés, H., 32, 39, 101, 146

Cortes (National Congress), 27, 28, 30, 31

Cortez, R., 141

Cosa, J. de la, 111

Côte d'Azur, *see* Riviera
Cruz, Ramón de la, 81
Cuba, 22, 26, 52, 65, 111, 112, 119, 120

Dalbor, J. B., 119, 147
D'Amicis, E., 119
D'Annunzio, G., 57, 130
Danube River, 119
Darnell, Linda, 140
Darwinism, 47
Daudet, A., 119
De Amicis, *see* D'Amicis
Del Río, A., 132
Desheredada, La, 134
Dickens, C., 134
Dominec, M., 140
Domínguez Barbera, M., 59, 141, 142, 148
Don Quixote, 7, 118, 121, 125, 134
Doña Perfecta, 76
Dumas, A., 20, 131
Dürer, A., 95

East Indies, 146
Echegaray, J., 120
Egypt, 39, 120
El Palmar, 65, 67
El Saler, 65
Ellis, H., 123
Entrambasaguas, J. de, 123, 130, 142, 148
Episodios Nacionales, 135
Escalante, M. A., 148
Europe, 20, 31, 73, 93, 145

Fabius, 63
Familia de León Roch, La, 76
Faust, 107
Félix, María, 97, 140
Fernández y Gonzáles, M., 20, 130, 131, 144
Ferrer, St. Vincent, 19, 25
First Republic, 22, 58
Flaubert, G., 47, 61, 122, 130
Ford, G., 94, 140
France, 21, 29, 35, 36, 38, 40, 41, 44, 71, 93, 94, 96, 97, 141, 145
France, A., 32
Franco, F., 41, 138

Franconia (ship), 39, 120
French Revolution, 23, 32
Freya (goddess), 96
Fuentes, A., 86
Fuerte Sarmiento, 101
Fuster, J., 141

Galdós, *see* Pérez
Galvez, B. de, 102
Garbo, Greta, 37, 60, 100
Gauls, 63
Gascó Contell, E., 8, 96, 121, 139, 140, 144, 145
Geneva, 31, 119
Genoa, 110
George Washington University, 37
Germany, 71, 93, 142
Germinal, 73, 74, 131, 143
Gibraltar, 80, 113, 115, 116
Giordano, U., 119
Goethe, J. W., 107
González Blanco, A., 47, 48, 67, 141-43
González Ruíz, N., 140
Gorki, M., 24
Goths, 33
Goya, F., 30, 68, 79, 81, 144
Gran Chaco, 34
Granada, 109
Grant, E. M., 143
Grao, El, 48
Greeks, 18, 62
Gulliver's Travels, 37, 104, 146

Hamilton, A., 144
Hannibal, 42, 60-64
Harding, W. G., 37
Hasnic, Count, 147
Havana, 24, 39
Hawaii, 39, 120
Hayworth, Rita, 140
Hegel, G. W. F., 134
Helen of Troy, 98, 100, 101, 107
Hemingway, E., 84
Herboso, Isabel, 111, 146, 147
Hercules, 62, 63
History of the French Revolution, 24
Hollywood, 35, 94, 97, 119
Holy Grail, 24
Homer, 98

Hong Kong, 120
Howells, W. D., 69, 123
Huerta, 52, 54, 58, 60, 114
Hugo, V., 24, 30, 36, 41, 48, 92, 119,
    121, 132, 133
Hurst, W. R., 39
Huysmans, J. K., 73

Ibáñez, F., 138
Ibáñez Martínez, Ramona, 18
Iberians, 62, 63
Ibiza, 80, 88, 89
Ibsen, H., 133
Ingram, R., 94
India, 39
Indians, 34, 116
Indies, 146
Intruse, L', 74
Irving, W., 24
Isabel II, Queen, 22, 65
Itálica, 61
Italy, 26, 29, 52, 108, 119, 140

Jaime I, 19, 24
Japan, 39, 120
Jason, 91
Java, 39, 120
Jerez de la Frontera, 69, 76, 77
Jesuits, 21, 73-75
Jews, 87, 89, 115, 144
Joan, Pope, 144
Jordan, Charlotte B., 36
Júcar River, 58, 60

Keniston, H., 144
König Friedrich August (ship), 93
Korea, 120
Kropotkin, P., 24, 71

La de Bringas, 73
League of Nations, 40
Lear, King, 119
Lee, Lila, 140
Legion of Honor, 31
León Roca, J. L., 8
Levi, E., 64
Life of Christopher Columbus, 24
Lilith, 107
Lilliput, 104, 105
Lima, 51

Liria, 20
Lisbon, 32, 91
Livy, 61
Llorca, F., 139
Llorente, T., 140
London, 71
Louisiana, 102
Louÿs, P., 61
Low Countries, The, 71
Luna, Pedro de, 39, 104, 106, 107
Lundeberg, O. K., 145
Lyons, 44

Macao, 120
Macrae, J., 36
Madame Bovary, 48, 64
Madoz, P., 141
Madras, 116
Madrid, 9, 17, 19, 20, 26, 28, 29,
    31-33, 53, 58, 59, 69, 71, 73, 76,
    78-80, 82-87, 91, 102, 119, 134,
    136, 141, 144, 147
Maeterlinck, M., 74, 133, 134, 143
Mallorca, 80, 87, 144
Manchuria, 120
Marne River, 94, 95, 133, 145
Marseilles, 97
Martínez, Vicenta, 19
Martínez Ruiz, J., *see* "Azorín"
Mas y Laglera, J., 146
Mascagni, P., 119
Masons, 21, 24
Mata Hari, 96, 145
Maupassant, G. de, 56, 113, 119, 133
Mediterranean Sea, 18, 36, 39, 48, 49,
    51, 52, 96, 97, 107, 118, 135, 136,
    140
Meistersinger, Die, 60
Melilla, 22
Menéndez Pidal, R., 137
Menton, 37, 38, 104, 106, 108-10, 123
Mérimée, P., 84
Mexican Revolution, 37, 118, 147
Mexico, 38, 39, 97, 101, 102, 112,
    119, 120, 139, 140
Michelet, J., 24
Milan, 58
Minotaur, 87
Misérables, Les, 133
Mobile, 102

Monaco, 98, 112
Monte Carlo, 98, 109, 112
Moors, 22, 109
Moreno, A., 100, 140
Morote, L., 82
Mozart, W. A., 71
Munich, 31, 119
Murger, H., 57

Naples, 58, 97, 119
Napoleon I, 22, 32, 82
National Library, Madrid, 9
New Carthage, 62
New World, 36, 38, 91, 93, 100, 101, 109-11
New York, 30, 39, 105, 120, 139, 140
Nietzsche, F., 24, 79, 147
Noah, 107
Nubia, 120
Nueva Valencia, 34, 35
Núñez de Balboa, V., 39

Odyssey, 52, 146
Ojeda, A. de, 39, 91, 104, 109-11, 135, 146
Old Wives' Tale, The, 48, 142
Ordóñez de Montalvo, G., 101
Ortúzar Bulnes, Elena, 40
Oteyzâ, L. de, 147

Pacific Ocean, 39
Padín, J., 139, 140
Palma (Mallorca), 87, 88
Panama, 39, 120
Paradou, 131
Paraguay, 32, 34
Pardales, Doctor, 144
Paris, 21, 22, 29, 35, 36, 38, 40, 53, 80, 83, 98, 100, 118, 133, 147
Pasadena, 105
Patagonia, 17, 33, 34, 99, 101
Pedralba, 20
Peñíscola, 107, 108
Pensacola, 102
Pérez Galdós, B., 17, 28, 73, 76, 84, 132, 134, 135, 144, 149
Peru, 39, 51, 145
Petronius, 62
Philadelphia, 37
Philippines, 23, 39, 120

Phoenicians, 18
Pi y Margall, F., 23, 27, 59
"Pigmalión," 138-40
Pinta (ship), 109
Pinzón, M. A., 109
Pitollet, C., 141, 148
Pizarro, F., 32, 39
Plato, 126
Plautus, 63
Poincaré, R., 95
Polybius, 61
Port Said, 116
Porter, Katherine A., 90
Portugal, 109
Power, T., 140
Prim, J., 65
Primo de Rivera, M., 29, 40, 120
Prometheus, 114
Proudhon, J., 71, 73
Puerto Rico, 23

Quo Vadis?, 61

Rabat, 115
Rabelais, F., 32
Ramón de la Cruz, *see* Cruz
Rascoe, B., 145
Reclus, J. J. E., 71
Renan, E., 24, 71
Revelation, Book of, 95
Rey, F., 97, 140
Rezanov, N. P., 39
Rhine River, 31
Ribeiro, M., 73
Río de Janeiro, 91
Río Negro, 33, 34, 99
Riviera, 17, 29, 37, 39, 40, 108, 112, 118, 120, 135, 137
Roca, *see* León
Romans, 18, 63, 96
Rome, 61-64, 108
Rosas y Reyes, R., 147
Rubens, Alma, 97, 140

Sagunto, 42, 60-63
San Francisco, 101, 102, 105
San Sebastián, 27, 53
St. Isidro, 78
St. John the Baptist, 19
St. Vincent Ferrer, *see* Ferrer

Salamanca, 132
Salammbô, 61, 130
Salaverria, J. M., 146
Salzburg, 31
Sand, George, 88, 89, 145
Santiago, Chile, 32, 139
Santo Domingo, 110, 111
Saragossa, *see* Zaragoza
Schopenhauer, A., 134
Scipio Africanus, 63
Scott, W., 20
Second Republic, 29, 41
Segovia, 20, 30
Sempere, F., 24, 31, 53
Seneca, 42
Sergas de Esplandián, Las, 101, 146
Serrano, F., 22
Seville, 29, 37, 61, 80, 85-87, 110
Shadow of the Cathedral, The, 148
Shakespeare, W., 119
Ship of Fools, 90
Siberia, 101
Sienkiewicz, H., 61
Silius Italicus, 61
Singapore, 120
Soler, D., 140
Soriano Barroeta-Aldamar, R., 27, 28, 59
Sorolla, J., 30, 43, 49
Soul of Spain, The, 148
South America, 29, 36, 90, 99, 108, 117, 118
Spain, 8, 9, 17, 20, 22, 23, 25, 29, 31, 35, 38, 60, 69-71, 73, 74, 91, 104, 109-11, 117, 120, 121, 135, 140, 142, 145, 149
Spanish America, 90, 104, 145
Spencer, H., 24
Starkie, W., 123
Stendhal, 124, 128
Switzerland, 40
Sudan, 39, 120
Swain, J. O., 68, 143
Swift, J., 104, 105, 146

Taine, H., 134
Tangiers, 115
Tannhäuser, 107
Teixeira, V., 140
Telemachus, 96

Temptress, The, 37, 100, 140
Tenerife, 91
Terres Maudites, 142
Terry, Alice, 14, 97, 140
Teruel, 18, 138
Teruel, Encarnación, 138
Theseus, 87
Thulin, Ingrid, 94, 140
Toilers of the Sea, 133
Toledo, 30, 69, 72-76
Tolstoi, L., 24, 64
Torrent, The, 37, 60, 140
Torrente Ballester, G., 147
Tribunal de las Aguas, 54
Triton, 96
Trojans, 98
Troy, 63
Turia River, 55
Turkey, 119

Ulysses, 96
Unamuno, M., 132
Unión Republicana, 25
United States, 8, 17, 23, 26, 37, 40, 41, 99, 103, 142
University of California (Berkeley), 100
University of Deusto, 75, 82
University of Madrid, 142
University of Rochester, 141
University of Valencia, 9, 19, 20, 138
Uruguay, 34

Valencia, 7, 9, 17-28, 31, 33, 36-38, 41-44, 46, 48, 49, 51, 52, 54, 57, 58, 60, 61, 64-66, 69, 76, 82, 123, 137-42, 149
Valentino, R., 35, 84, 94, 140
Valldemosa, 88
Valle-Inclán, R. del, 145, 146
Van Diemen's Land, 105, 146
Vanderbilt Unviersity, 10
Vega Carpio, L. F. de, 141
Velasquez, D., 47, 68
Venice, 31, 58
Venus, 107
Venusberg, 108
Vercher, 57
Vichy, 31, 119
Vienna, 119

Villa, F., 120
Virgin Mary, 25, 72, 111, 146
Visigoths, 18
Vives, J. L., 25
Vizcaya, 73, 75
Voronoff, Dr. S., 40

Wade, G., 10
Wagner, R., 27, 30, 32, 92, 95, 107, 119
War of 1870, 94
Washington, D.C., 37
Waterloo, 133
Wells, H. G., 136
West Indies, 33
West Point, 37

Wilson, W., 99
Winkler, P., 146
Woman Triumphant, 124
World War I, 8, 17, 29, 90, 93, 104, 117, 118, 128, 136
World War II, 95, 136

Zacinto, 62
Zamacois, E., 31, 57, 68, 129, 140, 142, 144
Zanetto, 119
Zaragoza, 133, 138
Zola, E., 21, 30, 38, 43, 46-48, 64, 73, 74, 119, 121, 130-34, 136, 143
Zurich, 31

DATE DUE

SE 23 '82	SEP 3 '82		
GAYLORD			PRINTED IN U.S.A.